Stories from
# NEW JERSEY
## *Diners*

Michael Gabriele

Stories from

# NEW JERSEY
## *Diners*

· · · · · · · · · · · · · · · · · · · · · · · · ·

Monuments to Community

MICHAEL C. GABRIELE

AMERICAN PALATE

Published by American Palate
A Division of The History Press
Charleston, SC
www.historypress.com

*Front cover image*: Three photos at top (*left to right*, all by M. Gabriele): Johnny Prince's Famous Bayway Diner, Linden; Park West Diner, Woodland Park; Summit Diner. Photo at bottom: Haledon Diner. *Courtesy Emily Diamond.* *Back cover images*: Kless Diner matchbook cover. *From the collection of Peter Lundell*; Mustache Bill's Diner (top right), Barnegat Light. *Photo by M. Gabriele*; Newton Diner (bottom). *Photograph from the collection of the Sussex County Historical Society, Newton.*

First published 2019

Manufactured in the United States

ISBN 9781467139823

Library of Congress Control Number: 2019943358

*Notice*: The information in this book is true and complete to the best of our knowledge. It is offered without guarantee on the part of the author or The History Press. The author and The History Press disclaim all liability in connection with the use of this book.

*"DINER"*

*I'm in a diner*
*Sittin' in a Jersey Diner*
*Because the neon lights are shinier*
*What the heck are they cooking, at a quarter to two (in the mornin')*

*A Jersey Diner*
*There's no place I'd rather be*
*Than sitting at the Tick Tock on Route 3*
*Eating chicken with the truckers and sipping coffee*

*Late at night, need a bite*
*Taylor Ham sandwich cooked just right*
*That's how much my diner means to me.*

*A Jersey diner*
*In the Iron Bound, or if you're a "piner"*
*The selection couldn't be finer*
*The left side of the menu for me*

*Lyrics © by David Rubin*
*Performed by the Swampgrass Jug Band*
*(sung to the melody of "Dinah," composed by Harry Akst, Sam M. Lewis and*
*Joe Young)*

Tick Tock Diner. *Photo by M. Gabriele.*

# CONTENTS

# ACKNOWLEDGEMENTS

Once again, for the fourth time, I would like to express my gratitude to my publisher, Arcadia Publishing and The History Press, and especially to my colleagues Katie Parry and J. Banks Smither, for giving me the opportunity to write a book about New Jersey history. This is my second book on the history of the Garden State's diner business.

I greatly appreciate the generosity of all the sources who are quoted throughout this text. They were kind enough to share their memories and experiences. I dedicate this book to them. Thank you to librarians and members of historical societies for your dedication and providing accurate research materials. Bravo to my son, Charles, for scanning many images used in this book.

My thanks goes to Richard Gutman, Larry Cultrera and John Baeder; Beth Lennon (Mod Betty); Phil DeRaffele of DeRaffele Manufacturing Company; Rich Rockwell of the Historical Society of Bloomfield; Sally Hastings, president of the Somers Point Historical Society; Al Brannen, president of the Wildwood Historical Society; Judge George Psak Jr.; members of the Summit Historical Society; Sandy Cannon; Barbara McAllister; Barbara Pickell, local historian librarian, Red Bank Public Library; Kathryn Rose Sylvester Fletcher; Mark Blasch; Richard A. Sauers, Riverview Cemetery historian; Marlene DeZurney Kwak; Mary Nelson, adult services librarian, Bound Brook Public Library; Linda Buset and Joe Baum; Richard Boas; Patricia Martinelli, administrator of Vineland Antiquarian and Historical Society; Mark W. Maxwell, president of the Egg

Harbor City Historical Society; Jacquelin Morillo, archivist, Atlantic City Free Public Library; Lisa Cohn, librarian, programming, special collections and reference, Bloomfield Public Library; author Paula Borenstein; Debra A. Zellner of Montclair State University; the Jewish Historical Society of New Jersey, based in Whippany; Ann Conway; Jacqueline LaPolla, Keyport Public Library; Margaret Lowden, Burlington County Library; Denise Wolf, Green Brook Historical Society; Peter Lundell; Bill Kless; Vic Bary, Cranford Historical Society; Al Beronio; members of the "Mt. Holly Area, Yesterday and Today" Facebook page; and members of the Weequahic High School Alumni Association.

*Notes from the author: All towns and cities mentioned in this book are located in New Jersey unless otherwise indicated. Several passages in this book contain information that previously appeared in articles (written by this author) in* The Record *newspaper and* New Jersey Monthly *magazine and on the website Jersey Bites.*

# "NOBODY EVER BRINGS ANYTHING SMALL INTO A DINER"

The Cornelius Low House Museum in Piscataway opened its doors for a "meet and greet" event on May 21, 2015, welcoming guests to "The History of New Jersey Diners" exhibit, a display of photos, artwork, factoids and original artifacts. This author, along with Richard J.S. Gutman, the dean of American diner history, served as co-curators for the exhibit, which had opened one month earlier.

An elderly woman and man were among the first to arrive for the reception. They smiled and conversed as they toured the displays. I approached them as they sat in one of the first-floor rooms, hoping that they would be eager to chat about the collection. But I noticed the man had his head bowed. His eyes were closed, and he placed his thumb and index finger on the bridge of his nose. He sobbed, whispered and gently shook his head: "The memories…it's too much, it's just too much." Clearly, he was overcome by the exhibit—the cumulative effect of the display and how diners were an important part of his life.

On May 31, 2017, a man awoke a few minutes after the stroke of midnight at his home in Charlottesville, Virginia. He got in his car and started driving north. Seven hours later, he arrived on Crooks Avenue in Paterson. His mission involved eating one last time at his favorite diner, the Egg Platter. Having relocated to Virginia, he had heard from relatives that this would be the final day of business for the Egg Platter. It had been announced that the diner, which opened in the 1940s, would be shuttered to make way for a new multipurpose building. Sitting at the counter on this early Wednesday

Egg Platter. *Photo by M. Gabriele.*

morning, he said that he grew up in Paterson and had many meals with his parents at the diner. Given the diner's impending demise, he felt compelled to drive 350 miles for a farewell breakfast.

SINCE 2013, THIS AUTHOR—DURING the course of numerous presentations at libraries, historical societies, museums and civic organizations throughout the state—has observed similar fervent reactions from a broad range of individuals when it involves contemplating a lifetime of diner memories. Diners and lunch wagons before them have been part of New Jersey life for 125 years. They're tied to the state's cultural identity. But why do diners resonate so strongly with Garden State residents? Why have diners become embedded in New Jersey's DNA?

Debra A. Zellner, PhD, a professor at Montclair State University's Psychology Department who studies the psychological dynamics of people and their consumption of food, said it's familiarity and a sense of belonging that causes people to form strong emotional bonds with diners. For Zellner, an academic study of food—what, how, where and why people eat—represents a fundamental part of human behavior that warrants serious scholarly exploration. "Diners are places where the community meets. It's the *Cheers* effect," she said, making a reference to the popular TV sitcom that ran from 1982 to 1993. "They're the places where you meet your friends for coffee. Customers know the people who own the diners. They know the waitresses."

The element of familiarity also plays into food selection for diner lovers. While many Jersey diners feature extensive, "phone book" menus, Zellner said that most people actually prefer fewer choices, relying on old favorites rather than experimenting with new selections. "People tend to like some choice, but not a lot. There can be choice 'overload' when it comes to dealing with a large menu. People usually focus on the familiar and get the 'regular' thing, even though they might appreciate the 'illusion' of many choices with a big menu." She said comfort food can bring back pleasant memories of special occasions with family and friends.

As for the underlying psychology, Zellner said that many segments of the population have various levels of anxiety and insecurity with the blistering pace of high-tech change they've seen over the last forty years. In contrast to this "future shock," diners represent a reliable, stable part of life. A diner's down-home charm, its lively atmosphere, familiar wait staff, décor, architecture and food all create a venue that eases the stress of life and sparks pleasure in the heart, mind, stomach and soul.

John Baeder—the acclaimed American artist whose paintings are featured in his 1978 book *Diners* and the 2015 book *John Baeder's Road Well Taken*—spoke about his affection for diners and the artwork that they inspire. Good art, he said, comes through the unconscious mind. Reflecting on his own inner artistic psychology, Baeder confessed that he's attracted to diners because, for him, they represent the "Great Mother" archetype. "Diners are warm, intimate meeting places; nourishment for the soul."

"When it comes to painting diner scenes, I consider myself to be more of a preservationist than an artist," he continued during a November 2018 phone interview. "Many of the diners I painted years ago are gone." As an observant customer, he's enchanted by what he calls the "diner dance," an invisible ballet that was revealed to him years ago at Curley's Diner in Stamford, Connecticut. This improvisational choreography involves movements and body language generated by short-order cooks, waitresses, cashiers and customers, all of which combine to create the diner's atmosphere.

Baeder grew up in Atlanta and came to the New Jersey/New York metropolitan area in 1964, when he worked as an art director at a Madison Avenue advertising agency. Once he arrived, he became fascinated by diners, guided by his aesthetic curiosity and thirst for adventure. "Diners were something new for me. On Sunday mornings, I would drive out to New Jersey. I didn't know where I was going, but I was making discoveries along the way. Diners found me as I traveled."

THE STORIES COLLECTED IN this book form a composite portrait of the Garden State's diner culture—a mosaic of the diner experience. These are remembrances that have shaped lives, families, careers, businesses and communities. Many tales are snapshots of the immigrant experience—people who have traveled to New Jersey from faraway countries to gain a foothold as American citizens. Other chapters reveal the journeys of people who have relocated from various corners of the United States, bringing with them their own regional food influences while expanding the choir of Jersey voices.

Diner history is intertwined with New Jersey history. As community monuments, diners stood as sentinels during the building of the Turnpike and the Parkway, secondary roads, bridges and tunnels; railroads and trolley lines; and factories and downtown business districts. Diners were there as farmlands, orchards and forests were cleared to make way for housing developments and sprawling shopping malls. They saw the rise, decline and rebirth of cities and towns. They watched the confident, soaring growth of regional industries as well as the tragic after-effects of deindustrialization.

People were sitting in their favorite diner, having lunch and drinking coffee, on November 22, 1963, when they heard that President John F. Kennedy had been assassinated. As a public forum, diners hosted heated discussions among customers on the Vietnam War and the Watergate controversy. Diner owners opened their doors to people reeling from the horror of September 11, providing a much-needed sanctuary for those who watched the collapse of the Twin Towers.

Diner experiences—good food, slice-of-life encounters with friends and strangers and the sentimental recollections they engender—have a larger-than-life, cinematic quality. These are the untold stories of New Jersey's history. The narrative is a tapestry of "everyday" life for "ordinary" people, where every day is meaningful and every person is significant with a heartfelt anecdote to share.

To better understand the poetry of all this, we can recall, with respectful apologies, the gentle, eloquent soliloquy by Elwood P. Dowd (played by James Stewart) in the classic 1950 movie *Harvey* and substitute diners for Elwood's preferred venue of bars as a sacred haunt to hear heroic American tales—the revealing, spontaneous conversations and personal confessions that provide a deeper understanding into life's many dramas. Diners are places where you spend quality time with a dear friend, someone just like Harvey:

*Harvey and I sit in diners and play the jukebox. And soon the faces of all the other people turn toward us and they smile. And they're saying: "We don't know your name mister, but you're a very nice fella." Harvey and I warm ourselves in all these golden moments. We've entered as strangers, but soon we have friends. And they come over and they sit with us and they talk to us. They tell about the big terrible things they've done and the big wonderful things that they'll do. Their hopes and their regrets and their loves and their hates—all very large, because nobody ever brings anything small into a diner.*

# STAINLESS STEEL REFLECTIONS

The Garden State holds the title of "Diner Capital of the World" for two reasons. First, New Jersey has more diners than anywhere else. Estimates from several sources range from five hundred to six hundred. Second, during the twentieth century, the Garden State was the diner *manufacturing* capital of the world. The business took root here. There once were more than twenty diner builders and renovators in the Garden State—companies like Kullman, Silk City, O'Mahony, Swingle, Mountain View, Paramount, Fodero, Master, Manno, Comac, Musi and Erfed. These were the "old masters." All of the state's diner builders have vanished. The business dynamics changed, and factory-built diners became a thing of the past.

The twentieth century was the golden era, when diners were prefabricated, modular, engineered structures, designed and built in factories and then shipped and assembled on a given site—near train stations, industrial zones, downtown business districts or choice spots on busy highways and byways. The website NorthJersey.com, on September 21, 2017, published an article that described diners as "icons" of New Jersey. They are examples of American industrial design and ingenuity, and their stainless steel panels reflect the history of the state.

During the 1930s, 1940s and 1950s, Jersey-built diners captured the distinctive Streamline Moderne architectural style, an outgrowth of the Art Deco movement and the American "Machine Age," which featured the design elements of sleek lines and aerodynamic forms, packaged with neon lights, glass bricks, marble countertops, terrazzo floors and decorative tile. The streamlined architectural concept extended to cars, locomotives, gas stations, apartment buildings and even kitchen appliances. The *New York Times*, in preview coverage of an exhibition at the Brooklyn Museum ("The Machine Age in America, 1918–1941") that appeared in its September 21, 1986 edition, reported:

> [T]*he idea of the Machine Age helped the nation understand and negotiate its rush from a predominantly rural, Protestant society to an urban, modern world of automobiles, radios and electric toasters….The Machine Age represents a distinctive period in art and design, forcing us to reconsider the shallow distinction we normally make between the exuberant 1920s* [the Jazz Age] *and the grim 1930s* [the era of the Great Depression]. *Artists and engineers, poets and advertising men, clergymen and secular intellectuals shared a reverence for the machine. A cheerful confidence, typified by the style known as streamlining—fluid lines, rounded contours, the image of speed and efficiency…unifies the period despite economic ups and downs.*

As part of this age of innovation, diners became the glistening, streamlined "machines" that fed hungry travelers, factory workers, truck drivers and middle-class families.

Phil DeRaffele, the patriarch of DeRaffele Manufacturing Company, a surviving golden age company, based in New Rochelle, New York, said the Garden State's superior infrastructure and road density carries an endless stream of hungry motorists "People in New Jersey love diners and the state is loaded with highways," he said. Years ago, this environment also attracted talent. DeRaffele said that when major diner builder P.J. Tierney Sons Inc. shuttered its New Rochelle operations in the early 1930s, many of the skilled tradesmen found work in New Jersey's growing diner manufacturing industry.

During the twentieth century, DeRaffele delivered many diners to customers in the Garden State, such as the original Ponzio's Diner in Cherry Hill and the Hightstown Diner. "I'm ninety years old," DeRaffele declared during a June 2018 phone interview. "Diners are still in my blood. I wake up early and come to work every day. I love it."

Diners in the twentieth century were an integral part of the post–World War II boom of mobile, car-happy Americans. Flowing into the 1950s, this was the period of a rapidly expanding middle class, suburban sprawl, interstate highways, rock-and-roll and the formative years of the baby boomer generation. Leisure time and disposable income were spent on family road trips. Teenagers and twentysomethings drawn to the romance of the open road inhabited diners on their journeys, which fed their wanderlust. Truck drivers had comfortable way stations to park their rigs and enjoy a good meal and friendly conversations.

The 1996 book *Hitting the Road: The Art of the American Road Map* stated that "as the population boomed [in the 1940s and 1950s]…American prosperity put at least one car in every driveway. Americans by the zillions were finding their way onto the road without the slightest provocation. By the late 1950s [interstate highways] had launched an entirely new generation of automotive travel in the United States, changing the face of the landscape."

The movement of restless motorists throughout New Jersey became the state's lifeblood and spawned the growth of diners as appealing, affordable places that served fresh, unpretentious American food, with "baking done on the premises." No reservations required. Wheels were turning, and the Garden State was being transformed into "the Corridor State." Historian and journalist John T. Cunningham, in his 1966 book *New Jersey: America's Main Road*, wrote:

> *New Jersey by the mid-1930s would enjoy a nationwide reputation for its good highways…no state carried a greater volume of traffic on its transportation arteries, whether that traffic be rail or motor. Truly, New Jersey is America's main road….By the time the automobile had begun to take over the pathway between New York and Philadelphia, New Jersey was being dubbed "the Corridor State."…Whatever the word of the moment, the passion of the nation, it has been reflected here. The reason is simple: people passed this way—colonialists, revolutionists, warriors, inventors, capitalists, workers, people of many nations and many races. They brought problems and they created answers.*

As people navigated New Jersey's roadways, bringing with them all their "problems and answers," they needed a place to take a break, sort things out and get a bite to eat. Diners fit the bill to accommodate them, but this was nothing new. The Garden State corridor has been providing hospitality to wayfarers and local residents ever since the seventeenth century. Long before there were diners on highways, taverns populated the state's old post roads and stagecoach routes and provided travelers with food, drink, entertainment and accommodations. Colonial taverns in New Jersey filled a niche similar to today's diners, as they were social centers for their communities—places where people would gather to eat, gossip, discuss business and tell tales about their long-distance journeys. Whether it's taverns in the 1700s and 1800s or diners in the twenty-first century, hospitality is a tradition that's ingrained in the Jersey state of mind.

Aside from their historical and architectural significance, New Jersey diners are a repository for nostalgia. They provide a setting for some of life's important moments, like a long-anticipated rendezvous that becomes a turning point in a relationship or a fond, simple remembrance of a meal among friends. Diners are the perfect place to unwind and top off a late night of carousing—a magnet for any number of strange individuals looking for a comfortable spot to land at 2:00 a.m.

But nostalgia has a double edge: the sweetness of warm, fuzzy recollections is set against the cold, sour reality that those days are long gone. Sometimes nostalgia focuses on memories of the diners themselves—the places that once were the centerpieces of halcyon days. Author Michael Chabon (*The Amazing Adventures of Kavalier and Clay*) in a March 25, 2017 online article for *The New Yorker* magazine, noted:

> *Nostalgia is a valid, honorable, ancient human emotion. The nostalgia that I write about, that I study, that I feel, is the ache that arises from the consciousness of lost connection. Nostalgia, most truly and most meaningfully, is the emotional experience—always momentary, always fragile—of having what you lost or never had, of seeing what you missed seeing, of meeting the people you missed knowing, of sipping coffee in the storied cafés that are now hot-yoga studios.*

While new diners have opened in recent years (such as JB's on 33 in Farmingdale, the Chit Chat in West Orange, the Majestic in Ramsey, the Metro in East Brunswick and the Maple Valley in Clifton), "storied" New Jersey eateries such as the Forum Diner in Paramus, the Elgin Diner in Camden, Mom's Diner in Avenel, the Excellent Diner in Westfield, the Lido Diner in Springfield and Rosie's Diner in Little Ferry have been torn down or relocated to make way for new highway construction projects, national franchise drugstores, fast-food chains, municipal redevelopment and maybe even a hot-yoga studio or two. The demise of these classic, factory-built diners has contributed to the Garden State's "consciousness of lost connection." Each diner had its place in a town's history, and each was tied to the collective memory of its respective community. Each had a loyal following of customers. This is how it goes. This is the business churn. But even when weighing a muted sense of loss, nostalgia serves as a reassuring reminder that diners are an essential part of New Jersey's spirit, character and mythology.

# "THE ROLLING, JINGLING, COFFEE-AROMA DISTRIBUTING LUNCH WAGON"

As documented in Gutman's book *American Diner Then & Now*, the ancestral origins of the modern diner date back to 1872, when Walter Scott steered his wagon through the streets of Providence, Rhode Island, to peddle coffee, sandwiches and hard-boiled eggs to passersby and factory workers. This street-level food distribution concept became popular as the "night lunch" business on city streets. Lunch wagons are the precursors to modern diners and the ancient ancestors of today's popular food trucks.

The Patrick J. Tierney Company in New Rochelle, New York, and the T.H. Buckley Car Manufacturing Company and Worcester Lunch Car and Carriage Manufacturing Company, both in Worcester, Massachusetts, were the leading producers of lunch wagons in the late 1800s and early 1900s. Gutman profiled the rise of the lunch wagon business in New England during the 1890s:

> *It was in Worcester* [Massachusetts] *that the lunch wagon business mushroomed into an industry. On September 1, 1891, Charles H. Palmer received the first patent given for a lunch wagon design. The patent described what was to become the standard configuration for nearly twenty-five years: the wagon had an enclosed body with the forward portion extending over a set of small front wheels, and the rear made narrower to stand between the tops of the high back wheels. The rear of the wagon was the "kitchen apartment" with a counter separating it from the dining room space, where stools or chairs could be installed. Over*

*one of the high rear wheels was a window for passing out food to those
customers standing on the curb; the other side had a carriage window, to
which you could drive up to place an order.*

The lunch wagon concept found a home in New Jersey, as well as other
states, representing the first wave of what was to become the modern diner
business. The book *Trenton Old and New* (updated and published under the
auspices of the Trenton Tercentenary Commission in 1964) had a chapter
on the completion of the state capital's municipal building on East State
Street in 1910. As explained in the book, the closing of the old municipal
building, which had been located at the corner of Broad and State Streets,
meant the loss of a popular institution:

> *Another familiar landmark, which disappeared when Trenton's
> municipal government moved to its new building on East State Street,
> was Peter G. Curtin's "pioneer" lunch wagon, which stood on Broad
> Street in front of the City Hall every night from 1894 to 1911. The
> original lunch wagon, built by Fitzgibbon and Crisp, and drawn by an
> unusually intelligent horse named Dandy, was later replaced by a new
> wagon, just as the original coffee and simple sandwiches gave way to a
> more elaborate menu. The lunch wagon hours were usually from 9:00
> p.m. to 4:30 a.m., one of its busiest periods being when the crowds
> from the Taylor Opera House stopped by for a snack while awaiting the
> last trolley home.*

An article in the February 1, 1914 edition of the *Trenton Evening Times*
reported that Curtin, identified as a "pioneer street caterer," had decided
to retire "with a comfortable bank roll…from selling frankfurters and other
food to hungry pedestrians at night." As a young man, Curtin worked
at the Singer Sewing Machine Company's manufacturing plant in the
Elizabethport section of Elizabeth, along Newark Bay, during the 1880s
(the Singer plant, located on a thirty-two-acre campus, opened in 1872).
The *Evening Times* article quoted Curtin as saying that he "saw that men
operating lunch wagons in Elizabeth made money and he decided to come
to Trenton to try his luck in the same line."

Curtain was referring to horse-drawn "freight wagons" that parked in the
cobblestone courtyard of the Singer plant to serve workers during the lunch
hour. This scene is captured in a postcard photo postmarked "Elizabeth,
June 9, 1911," written in German by a woman named Ida to her friend

Intersection of Broad and State Streets, Trenton, circa 1890. *Courtesy Trenton Public Library.*

Liebe. "I have been very business with sewing [presumably a reference to working at Singer]. Hope you are well."

The postcard photo shows workers congregating around four wagons in the Singer courtyard, one of which sold "Mrs. Wagner's Famous Homemade Pies." According to information on the website oceangrovehistory.org, posted on August 26, 2015, Mrs. Wagner started her business in the 1870s, baking fruit pies in a wood stove from her home on Webb Avenue in the seaside resort town of Ocean Grove. She purchased fresh fruit, milk, eggs, flour and pig's lard from nearby farms in Monmouth County. Her business grew, and by the early 1900s, Mrs. Wagner had established bakeries in Newark and Jersey City—in proximity to the Singer plant.

A story in the May 6, 1928 *Trenton Sunday Times-Advertiser* offered additional insights on how Curtain first hatched his career as a lunch wagon proprietor:

> [Curtin] *was working as a machinist in the Singer Sewing Machine Company's plant in Elizabeth when the first lunch wagon there began*

Freight wagons, Singer courtyard, 1911. *Courtesy Richard Gutman.*

*to stop at the plant. Striking up an acquaintance with the owner of the Elizabeth wagon, Mr. Curtin had an opportunity during a week's vacation to operate the wagon while his friend sought respite from the daily grind. The taste of the business thus acquired determined Curtin to establish a lunch wagon of his own. Since Elizabeth was already supplied with such service it was necessary to find an opening elsewhere and investigation led Curtin to Trenton where relatives lived. He secured a license to operate such a wagon on the streets and then had one build by Fitzgibbon and Crisp. It was a familiar sight to see Peter Curtin drive downtown each evening at about 8:30 or 9:00 o'clock, unhitch his horse and send him to a livery stable, and enter upon a brisk trade. There was always a delegation of the hungry and thirsty awaiting him…and Curtin always had plenty of sandwiches and hot coffee ready for them.*

Wagon production and the design expertise that went with it were well established in New Jersey during the late 1800s. The Paterson Wagon Company (later to be known as the Paterson Vehicle Company and the builder of Silk City diners) operated in the Silk City. Elizabeth was home to several wagon manufacturing companies during the nineteenth century, according to Robert J. Baptista's 2015 book *Elizabeth, New Jersey: Then and Now.* In addition to freight wagons providing food at the Singer plant, Baptista wrote that there were milk delivery wagons that operated in Elizabeth (the city had thirty-one milk dealers in 1919), while a family seafood market "used a horse and wagon to sell fish, oysters and clams throughout the city."

"Coming to Trenton…and noting there was not a lunch wagon to be seen anywhere in the city, [Curtin] hired the carriage maker Fitzgibbon and Crisp to construct a wagon with which he realized his dream," Richard A. Sauers, Riverview Cemetery historian, wrote in his 2015 blog spot "Trenton's First Lunch Wagon."

Curtin purchased a lunch wagon from Fitzgibbon and Crisp in 1894, and "before long he was selling coffee, pies and sandwiches from it at night" from a spot in downtown Trenton "near the smokestack of the old State Gazette Building," the 1914 *Trenton Evening Times* article stated. "Many persons passed his wagon and they were not long in discovering that the food sold by him was clean, well prepared and always fresh. Every night for seventeen years the wagon stood there, its business all the time growing, until along came the edict that he must move away."

He acquired a second wagon and maintained his business at several locations in Trenton before deciding to retire. "I suppose that I made the most money selling frankfurters," he said, quoted in the 1914 *Times* story. "A 'hot doggie' as they call them with a little mustard on it and inside a split roll seemed to hit the right spot with the multitude."

Trenton's "pioneer street caterer" had become such a legendary figure that he garnered a full-page story in the May 6, 1928 *Trenton Sunday Times-Advertiser*, referenced earlier. The eight-column banner headline "City's First Lunch Wagon Now Memory" topped a sentimental feature that looked back on Curtin's accomplishments. It also provided a behind-the-scenes look at the lunch wagon business and traced the growth of the business ever since Curtin said goodbye to his patrons:

> *Since Peter started his business…many lunch wagons have sprung up in Trenton, but none of them play so important a role as did the dinky, crowded car that rolled nightly into its place at Trenton's crossroads. Peter's wagon was the forerunner of its kind here. There are much larger wagons now, with shining tile and nicked fittings, scattered around the city in strategic places where sandwiches and lunch counter service are in demand. Most of them are built to a standard pattern…[and] depend on city gas, electricity, water and even have sewer connections. Gone is the romance from the lunch wagon business. The rolling, jingling, coffee-aroma distributing lunch wagon…has gone for good.*

The lunch wagon business became the focal point for the Curtin family, according to the 1928 article. "Curtin's wagon provided him with the means to raise nine children. Mrs. Curtin baked pies and beans, made two big pans of rice pudding every day, and did much of the purchasing and supervision of the wagon while it was being prepared for the night's trade. As the children grew large enough to assume various tasks, each had a part of the work assigned as a daily chore." The story also paid tribute to Curtin's horse, Dandy. "Curtin had an unusual horse in Dandy, the steed which hauled his wagon year after year. Dandy loved to parade through the streets with his gaily decorated car behind." Dandy understood many verbal commands from Curtin and knew the route, the various stops to serve customers and the way home.

Born on October 17, 1859, in Brooklyn, New York, Curtin died at age seventy-four on November 15, 1933, and is buried at Trenton's historic Riverview Cemetery, as documented by Sauers.

Fitzgibbon and Crisp's Union Carriage Works, a major manufacturing company in Trenton, built Curtin's first lunch wagon. The 1882 book *Industries of New Jersey: Trenton, Princeton, Hightstown, Pennington and Hopewell* (Part 1: *Industries of New Jersey*) had a description of the Trenton wagon builder, which housed its manufacturing operations on Bank Street:

> In the best work of fine carriage making, remarkable for elegance of finish and originality of design, combined with lightness, strength and durability, Messrs. Fitzgibbon and Crips, proprietors of the Union Carriage factory, are the most noted manufacturers in Trenton. This factory was originally established in 1868 by Messrs. Cadwallader, Wood and Company. Mr. Wood retired from the firm in 1874 and Mr. Fitzgibbon was admitted to fill the vacancy. In 1877 Mr. Cadwallader retired from the firm and Mr. Crisp was admitted to full partnership with Mr. Fitzgibbon. They build all kinds of light family carriages, from the light track sulkey to the stately coach, and from a light grocer's wagon to the heaviest truck, also rockaways, phaetons, buggies…[and] a large number of platform-spring market wagons. Employment is given to a large number of experienced and skilled workmen and they turn out upwards of 150 fine carriages and buggies per annum.

Not long after Curtin stepped down from his Trenton lunch wagon business, a man named Ted Forker opened a lunch wagon on Perry Street in Trenton. A story in the August 11, 1946 edition of the *Sunday Times-Advertiser* reported that Forker's "opening night" began just after the clock struck midnight on New Year's Day 1918, "when he was swamped with customers until daylight." In the article, Forker reminisced about his twenty-eight years of business, saying he had purchased the lunch wagon from "a man who used to operate it at the Victor Talking Machine plant in Camden."

An online version of the journal *Historical and Industrial Review of Camden, New Jersey*, published in 1890, listed five wagon builders in the city. A short page-one news item in the April 11, 1901 edition of the *Camden Daily Courier* reported that a lunch wagon, located at the intersection of Federal and Arch Streets, had "passed into new ownership," revealing that this business was in place and operating prior to this date. The owner, presumably, was a Camden entrepreneur named Arthur J.E. Morin. The newspaper also identified Howard Robinson as the lunch wagon's "popular night manager." In subsequent years, newspaper coverage indicated that even though the lunch wagon enjoyed a strong following in downtown Camden, the business—referred to in news stories simply as "the lunch wagon"—occasionally clashed with city hall officials and neighborhood merchants. Apparently, the wagon, which measured sixteen feet and two inches in length, was viewed by some as hindrance for plans to redevelop the neighborhood.

Morin died at the age of forty-one on June 14, 1915, due to complications from various illnesses. His obituary stated that in addition to the lunch wagon at Arch and Federal, he owned a second wagon at the intersection of Front Street and Kaighn Avenue. A year earlier, Robinson had left the business and, on May 2, 1914, opened a "lunch room" on the corner of Fifth and Arch Streets.

Forker, in the 1946 *Times-Advertiser* story, was quoted as saying that he enjoyed his "big years" when he operated his wagon at Trenton's Pennsylvania Railroad "Coalport" yard. "Many of the train crews terminating their day's work at the yards would head for Forker's wagon for a bite to eat before retiring. Ted would get the same crews for breakfast on their return to work the next day." Linda J. Barth, in her book *The Delaware and Raritan Canal* (Images of America), wrote that the Coalport yard was a railroad hub adjacent to the kilns of the Enterprise Pottery production plant. Barth said Trenton was a pottery manufacturing center, with "more than fifty companies at its zenith in the 1920s." The train yard would have given Forker access to plenty of hungry customers. Forker most likely learned how to cook from his dad, who managed a restaurant at Trenton's old Inter-State Fairgrounds, which opened in 1888, according to the *Times-Advertiser* article.

THE CHARTER OF THE City of Paterson, a municipal document published in 1908, spelled out the ordinances and guidelines for properly operating a lunch wagon in the Silk City:

> *Any person desiring permission to maintain any lunch wagon on any street shall make application to said Committee on Licenses, which application shall contain the full name, place of residence, and occupation of the application, and the place or places where he wishes to locate said wagon or wagons, and no license shall be granted to any person to maintain any wagon within four-hundred feet of any other licensed lunch wagon. Every applicant for such concession must have the indorsement of four citizens of the City of Paterson as to his character. The fee for such license shall be fifty dollars for each wagon, per annum. All ordinances inconsistent with the provisions of this ordinance are hereby repealed. Passed March 6, 1905; approved March 9, 1905.*

Henry "Night Owl" McCabe owned a popular horse-drawn lunch wagon in downtown Passaic, located at the corner of Main Avenue and Washington Place, during the mid-1890s. The *Passaic Daily News* carried a story ("Night Owl McCabe's Wrath"), noting that he "hopped about on his perch like a crazy bird" on the night of Thursday, February 28, 1895, when six "sportive youths" began pulling his lunch wagon up Main Avenue. He had been attending to his "many hungry customers" that evening when the wagon began moving unexpectedly. "McCabe said some fearful things and made a jump for the door. His customers were enjoying the joke and the ride. The motive power vanished before McCabe could find out who was teasing him. He had to draw the wagon back to Washington Place all by himself and every foot of the way the passersby were treated to new and wonderful forms of profanity."

According to his newspaper clippings, McCabe was a local celebrity and politically active in Passaic. An article in the September 19, 1933 edition of the *Herald-News* recapped his career. "Henry McCabe, present exalted ruler of the Passaic Lodge of Elks, came to Passaic in 1895 and opened his Palais Royal. All day, in her kitchen, Mrs. McCabe cooked the food and then toward evening the wagon was loaded and drawn to its corner by horse power. Sandwiches, hot Boston beans (the best!), cold chicken legs, pies and coffee were sold. At times the profits were $1,000 a month. He went out of business in 1912."

The pages of the *Elizabeth Daily Journal*, during the late 1890s and early 1900s, contained numerous stories that mention lunch wagons, but most of these reports involved robberies, police activities, disorderly individuals or portraying the mobile eateries as being an unwelcomed nuisance. Aside from Elizabeth, the datelines for these articles included the towns of Rahway, Plainfield, Garwood and Cranford, which indicates that lunch wagons were a common sight during this period.

A page-one story in the *Journal*'s May 23, 1906 edition published an entertaining tale involving a lunch wagon. The one-column headline and subheads offered a delicious preview: "Midnight Wedding in a Lunch Wagon; Couple, Eloping in an Automobile, Made Man and Wife by Negro Minister; Second Auto in Pursuit; Patron of the Lunch Wagon Stops Munching a 'Hot Dog' to Act as Witness." This marriage took place during the midnight hour at a lunch wagon owned by Edward Flynn, located at Elizabeth and Rahway Avenues.

The love-struck young couple, believed to be from Rutherford, stopped their car and went into the lunch wagon to ask where they might find a clergyman to perform an impromptu, off-hour wedding ceremony. By chance, an African American minister was having a late-night snack at the mobile eatery and made his presence known to the elopers. "I'm a minister of the Gospel," he announced. "I am the Reverend John Gaines of Wilmington, Delaware." The couple had a marriage document in their possession, and wedding vows were made on the spot. Flynn served as one witness, while a hot dog munching patron named James Sheridan signed the marriage document as a second witness.

The happy couple jumped back into their car and sped away. Moments later, another car pulled up next to the lunch wagon. A man and woman, frantic relatives of the just-married couple, barged into the lunch wagon and asked a flurry of questions, one of which no doubt included "Which way did they go?" They ran back to their car and "rode off after the couple at breakneck speed." It was just another night at a lunch wagon in Elizabeth. Stuff like this only happens in New Jersey.

The July 15, 1910 edition of the *Progressive Age*, a New York business journal that reported on developments in gas, electricity and water utilities, carried a news item on the opening of "the largest and most elaborate lunch wagon in the United States." Built by John J.E. Hennigan of Worcester, Massachusetts, and owned by F.J. Millward, the lunch wagon was located at the corner of Clinton Avenue and Maple Street in West Hoboken (today's Union City). Hennigan manufactured Franklin lunch wagons in Worcester

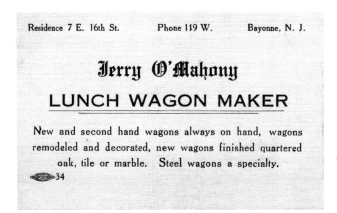

Residence 7 E. 16th St.      Phone 119 W.      Bayonne, N. J.

# Jerry O'Mahony
## LUNCH WAGON MAKER

New and second hand wagons always on hand, wagons remodeled and decorated, new wagons finished quartered oak, tile or marble. Steel wagons a specialty.

34

Jerry O'Mahony's business card. *Courtesy Barbara Marhoefer and the Jerry O'Mahony Archives.*

from 1907 to 1917. Millward's West Hoboken wagon measured twelve by thirty-two feet in width and length, with an interior height (floor to the midway point of its barrel-roof ceiling) of nine feet. It had a seating capacity of thirty (two parallel rows of circular stools at two separate eating counters), a price tag of $3,500 and a counter of white Italian marble with a tiled floor. "The wagon is equipped with both electric and gas lights, also water and telephone, and is always open." The article pointed out that the wagon made use of the latest modern gas cooking appliances, such as a two-burner hot plate, a broiler and griddle, a six-pot steam table and warming closet, coffee urns, a single-oven gas range, a three-burner stove with a canopy and a double oven for pastry work.

Jerry O'Mahony of Jerry O'Mahony Inc., a founding father of New Jersey's diner history, built his first lunch wagon in the backyard of his Bayonne home, which was located at 7 East Sixteenth Street, and sold it to an entrepreneur named Michael J. Griffith. A July 3, 1912 contract signed by Griffith stated that the lunch wagon would be located in West Hoboken (Union City) at a confluence of boulevards and trolley lines once known as "Transfer Station." In the mid-1920s, O'Mahony moved to a factory in Elizabeth and became one of the foremost diner manufacturers. O'Mahony diners operating today in New Jersey include the Summit Diner, the Broad Street Diner in Keyport, the Horizon Diner at the intersection of Routes 9 and 50 in Manahawkin and the Royal Diner on Route 31 in Washington.

O'Mahony wrote an article ("Eating on Wheels") for the December 1921 edition of *The American Restaurant* magazine, in which he described lunch wagons as a lucrative business venture for forward-thinking individuals. He also provided details on the design and construction of his lunch wagons,

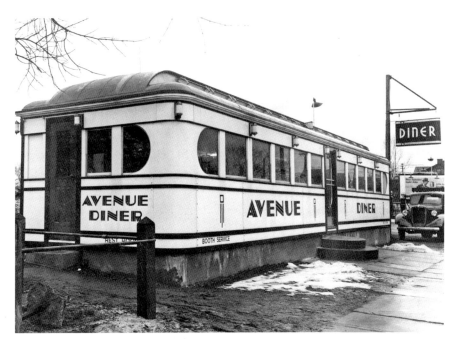

Avenue Diner, built by O'Mahony, circa 1938. *Courtesy Barbara Marhoefer and the Jerry O'Mahony Archives.*

saying that each one was built to meet the building code requirements of their respective localities. "Our car [interior] is all tile and quartered oak, interior finish furnished with skylights, screens and steps and mounted on a heavy running gear."

In an assignment designed to capture the essence of this burgeoning lunch wagon business and its clientele, the February 7, 1926 edition of *The New York Times Magazine* section reported that "here gathered night workers with an hour to spend in eating and chatting, the night owl who sought sustenance before turning in, and he who had no place into which he might turn. In the lunch wagon atmosphere, one might hear the views of the man in the street on vital questions—anything and everything from the crossword puzzle craze to the view of Conan Doyle [the creator of Sherlock Holmes] and Sir Oliver Lodge [a British physicist] on life after death and spiritual phenomenon. Here gathered the satirist, humorist, raconteur, and over a post-prandial [the period after a meal] cup of coffee offered leisurely contribution to the discussion."

This story described the atmospherics of New York City lunch wagons and the intelligentsia that they attracted, but the same observations would have applied to the mobile eateries across the Hudson River. The feature article also discussed the role of the lunch wagon proprietor who "had to possess other gifts than technical ability in the short-order line. He must know a little of most things, from the price of the Kentucky Derby favorite and baseball statistics, to the latest popular book that had been put into the movies."

The August 21, 1926 edition of the *Times* ran an article about a young lunch wagon operator in Princeton named Howard Fogelsong. The story indicated that Fogelsong had been denied admission to Princeton University in the fall of 1925. Undeterred, Fogelsong, apparently an enterprising individual, opened a lunch wagon on University Place within the campus environs. Students referred to his eatery as "Fogie's Lunch." The story stated that "for a short time he [Fogelsong] attended a local school, but later gave up his studies to develop all his energies to his growing business." His dedication paid off, and he opened another lunch wagon in Kingston.

A story in the January 8, 1928 *Sunday New York Times* business section reported that Samuel H. Kullman and James Moran signed a long-term lease for a large section of a one-story building in Newark, located on Empire Street between Frelinghuysen Avenue and Mechanic Street. "The lessees will manufacture lunch wagons and dining cars," the story stated. By the mid-1930s, the Kullman Dining Car Company had moved to Harrison and later opened facilities in Avenel and Lebanon. Kullman spanned three generations of family ownership over eight decades.

FAINT TRACES OF THE evolution of early diners from lunch wagons can be found at several locations throughout the state. Amy's Omelette House (the Burlington Diner), Plum on Park, Montclair and the Dumont Crystal Diner rank as New Jersey's oldest diners. For this author, the designation of "oldest diner" refers to the age of the existing diner car as it stands today, not any earlier iterations or overall lineage.

The Burlington Diner on Route 130 opened in 1927, according to Chris Stratis, whose family members worked at the diner. Stratis said his identification of the date is part of his family's history. An article in the February 6, 1983 edition of the *Courier Post* reported that the diner began as a "dining car on wheels in 1927," owned by members of the Stratis and Mastoris families. The present-day front dining hall, which faces High Street, was added in 1959. Phil DeRaffele, in a separate interview, concurred with Chris Stratis, saying that the first car was manufactured in

1927 by P.J. Tierney, where his father, Angelo, was a foreman. The second car arrived in the early 1930s, this time built by DeRaffele, the company started by Angelo. The Burlington Diner enjoyed its peak years following World War II and maintained a twenty-four-hour operation. These were the boom years for the Burlington area, as it became a center for toy, shoe and industrial pipe manufacturing.

Chris Stratis, in 1984, bought his father John Stratis's ownership stake and acquired additional family shares in 1998 and 2001. Stratis said that he learned the basics of diner business through his father and relatives during his years of apprenticeship at the Burlington Diner. "It was like being in a university," he said. "I grew up in the business. Diner work was perfect for me. I learned how to cook, but I also learned about the economics of the business."

Stratis identified Howard Broadbent as the most memorable character at the Burlington Diner. Broadbent, who carried the nickname "Junior," started working as a waiter at age fourteen. He soon became a local legend, famous for his photographic memory and rapid service. The February 6, 1983 edition of the *Post* lionized Broadbent as the diner's celebrity in residence. "Howard, know to all as Junior, has been a busboy, waiter and head waiter for forty years. Orders stick to Broadbent's brain the way hash browns stick to an ungreased pan. Junior does not even bother to write them down."

Burlington Diner. *Courtesy Chris Stratis.*

Amy's Omelette House (Burlington Diner). *Photo by M. Gabriele.*

In August 2004, Stratis sold the business to Amy's Omelette House. What was the best part of the diner ownership experience for Stratis? "The customers," he answered. "My customers were all good people. Families came to the diner [over the years] and I watched the kids grow up."

There is documentation that reveals the date of birth for the Park Diner (known today as Plum on Park), located at 14 Park Street in Montclair. Beneath the stylish wooden front entrance and brick exterior of Plum on Park lurks the heart of a diner built by O'Mahony. The 1930 Montclair City Directory, housed in the reference department of the Montclair Public Library, lists a "restaurant" owned by John Cestone. There is no mention of the place in the 1929 directory. Additional listings for Cestone's restaurant at 14 Park Street were found in the 1931 and 1932 directories. The 1929 Field Tax Map of Montclair (Map 37, Block K, Lot 21, which corresponds to the Park Avenue location) identifies a June 1, 1929 deed by a grantee, a New Jersey corporation named the Ideal Dining Car Company Incorporated, for the "lease of a dining car." Julius and Anna Wolff are listed as the grantors or property owners. The deed, recorded on June 24, 1929, makes reference to the dining car as an "out building" that measured fifty-five feet by sixteen feet—the same dimensions of today's Plum on Park (not counting the entrance or the subsequent kitchen addition). The value of the property in the 1929 deed, which includes the worth of the dining car, is given as $8,100.

An article in the November 4, 1943 edition of the *Montclair Times* reported on the early days of the Park Diner. The story indicated that the ownership team of Archie Ferguson and Homer Daniels acquired the diner in 1935. The news was that due to lack of manpower, the diner was forced to curtail its twenty-four hour/seven day a week schedule. "Fourteen years ago the diner opened its doors for business," the story stated. "Until Saturday night [October 30] it had never closed." Instead of a "one hundred sixty eight hour" weekly affair, the diner would open at 6:00 a.m. and close "at the dinner hour," much to the disappointment of its hamburger-loving, night-owl patrons. "There were some disappointed people at Park Street and Bloomfield Avenue Saturday night. They were hungry, too. They had come to the Park Diner for a snack before retiring, but found it closed for the first time in its history."

Bill Mandros became the owner of the Park Diner in 1978. He decided to sell the place during the summer of 2000. The diner changed hands several times and once was known as the Market Restaurant. Natalie Colledge took charge in October 2010 and currently operates the eatery as an upscale bistro. Colledge renovated the interior in 2018.

The Dumont Crystal Diner is located at 45 West Madison Avenue in its namesake Bergen County town. The tax clerk for the borough of Dumont provided a tax document that notes the diner was constructed in 1920, but this undoubtedly refers to an earlier eatery at the same address. Interviewed for an article penned by this author, published in the January 30, 2017 edition of *The Record* newspaper, Gutman explained that the date on the tax document wouldn't correspond to the existing Dumont Crystal, as it was built by O'Mahony "no earlier than 1928 and possibly around 1932. It could very well be that the diner replaced a [separate] lunch wagon that was on the same site." The existence of such a lunch wagon would explain the 1920 tax document.

"Too often, the date of the first incarnation is subsequently claimed [forever] as the date when an existing diner was built," Gutman said. "The Dumont Crystal is too wide to have been built before the mid-1920s at the earliest, based upon my scrutiny of the O'Mahony catalogs in my collection." He determined that the Dumont Crystal is most likely a "Victory Dining Car" in the O'Mahony line built in the early 1930s.

Lutfi (Louie) Saleh, who was born in the ancient city of Bethlehem in the Middle East, is the current owner of the Dumont Crystal. Saleh came

Dumont Crystal Diner. *Photo by M. Gabriele.*

to the United States on January 29, 1983, and worked as a line cook at the Tick Tock Diner in Clifton. In 2014, Saleh bought the diner from Momir Saranovic, who had come to America from Yugoslavia in December 1967 and started working at the diner in 1975.

The diner sits adjacent to the tracks of the "West Shore Line" of the old New York Central Railroad. The name of the nearby side street that runs perpendicular to the diner is West Shore Avenue, which refers to the now-defunct passenger train line. The tracks are still used by freight trains. The train carried passengers and railroad employees who ate at the diner. There were three distinct Dumont railroad stations that were located adjacent to the diner. The first, the Schraalenburgh station (Dumont originally was incorporated as the borough of Schraalenburgh), opened in 1883, was renamed the Dumont station in 1894 and then burned down in 1912. The second, a freight house, was used from 1912 to 1917. The third station was built in 1917 and operated until passenger service ceased in December 1959. It was abandoned and then torn down. Today, a pharmacy sits on the site of the third station.

Janet Earley Manning, a writer from Old Tappan, said that her mom, Olive (everyone called her "Kay"), was a "little red-headed spitfire" who worked at the diner as a waitress. Her grandfather William Earley Sr., a veteran of World War I, was the station master and ticket agent at the Dumont station and a frequent patron of the diner for breakfast and lunch.

Dumont train station, circa 1950. *Courtesy Newt Sweet.*

Newt Sweet (Dumont High School class of 1966), a retired train engineer and local historian, started his career on the railroad as a runner of errands for the local station master. He began working full time for the railroad in 1970 and nearly every morning had breakfast at the Dumont Crystal. He remains a frequent patron today. As an eleven-year-old, he rode the final passenger train from Weehawken to Dumont on December 10, 1959.

Mary (Corcodilos) Mastoris, the matriarch of the grand Mastoris diner and banquet hall located on Route 130 in Bordentown, when interviewed in 2012, recalled when she and her family took the train to Hightstown from Perth Amboy on a Sunday in the spring of 1927 to meet with Jerry O'Mahony to discuss plans to open a new diner. Mary was six years old at the time. Hightstown was virgin territory and mostly farmlands, but O'Mahony had picked out a spot on Old Route 33 (Mercer Street), adjacent to the town's train station.

Nicholas Corcodilos (Mary's father) purchased a twelve-stool O'Mahony lunch wagon and opened for business in 1927, which evolved into the Hightstown Diner. The Hightstown Diner, currently under the ownership of the Antonellos family, celebrated the ninetieth anniversary of its lineage with a birthday party on February 16, 2017.

The O'Mahony lunch wagon was removed to make way for the current Hightstown Diner car, built in 1941 by DeRaffele. Mary Mastoris, in her

Hightstown Diner. *Photo by M. Gabriele.*

memoir, wrote that in 1940 the family decided it was time to consider "a new concept in diners. Carl Johnson of New Rochelle was an airline designer and had changed his profession to designing dining cars. He brought us a rendering of a modern, all–stainless steel exterior and interior diner. Our grand opening brought people from all over to see this very modern eatery. Our menu became a little more sophisticated; along with turkey and veal we now included steaks, chops, fresh seafood, roast prime rib of beef, lamb, and a larger variation of desserts. For the first time we hired women waitresses because [World War II] had just begun and male employees were unavailable."

The Summit Diner opened in its namesake Union County town in 1938. The diner was predated by two lunch wagons that go back to 1904–5. (See the section "Haircuts on Maple Street.")

THE GROWTH OF TODAY'S gourmet and ethnic specialty food trucks represents a full-circle moment in the Garden State's mobile food tradition. The plucky motorized chefs who own these colorful vehicles are, quite literally, following in the wheel trails of lunch wagons that plied their trade more than a century ago. Today's food truck vendors fit the same profile of their lunch wagon ancestors: they are free-spirit entrepreneurs who enjoy owning their own business; they like to cook, work with their hands and are energized by their customers. Success for today's food truck operators is measured in their creativity, engaging personalities and the ability to produce tasty burgers, tacos, sandwiches, smoothies, falafels, empanadas, gyros, kimchee, salads and desserts. Hot dog vans and pushcarts also are longtime staples of the Garden State's roadside dining experience.

Rutgers University's "Grease Trucks," which became famous on the New Brunswick campus, represent a distinct species of food trucks in the Garden State's mobile food network. According to various online articles and information posted on the RU Hungry website, grease truck history dates back to the late 1970s and the creation of the "fat sandwich," an extra-large roll stuffed with meat (beef or chicken), French fries, cheese, lettuce and tomatoes. The original nine trucks were operated and owned by Vietnam veterans. Ayman Elnaggar and his "RU Hungry" vehicle, in 1997, became one of the early purveyors of fat sandwiches and grease truck fare at Rutgers.

Beginning in 2013, there was a shift at Rutgers regarding the licensing of grease trucks, as reported in the university newspaper, the *Daily Targum,* and other media outlets. According to the university's Institutional Planning

Cubano X-Press Food Truck, Jersey City. *Photo by M. Gabriele.*

and Operations Department, there were four "mobile food vendors" as of December 2018 with permits to operate on the New Brunswick campus. "We have no more grease trucks," a department spokeswoman said. In late 2016, Elnaggar reinvented RU Hungry and opened it as a kiosk in a building on Hamilton Street.

A defining moment for New Jersey food truck operators came after Hurricane Sandy pummeled the state on October 29, 2012. Jon Hepner, who drives his Aroy-D (translated as "very yummy") Thai Elephant food truck, along with a number of his food truck associates, answered a call to duty in the wake of the storm—a plea from residents in Hoboken and towns along the Jersey Shore—to feed people who had lost power and suffered major storm damage. Food trucks had the mobility and flexibility to reach people battered by the storm, Hepner said. It was this gallant effort that inspired the formation of the New Jersey Food Truck Association (NJFTA).

The mission of the NJFTA, founded in March 2013, is to establish a support network for the state's food trucks, define "best business practices," organize events, encourage new vendors to enter the field and advocate on behalf of members to help them understand the many safety and health codes, municipal ordinances and state regulations that affect the food truck business. Hepner, the founder and president of the NJFTA, said the organization maintains an alliance with the Philly Mobile Food Association of Philadelphia.

Dandy, Peter Curtin's intelligent horse, would be pleased that the legacy of lunch wagons lives on in today's diners and food trucks. In fact, Dandy was so smart that he probably knew all along how things would pan out.

# NORTHERN NEW JERSEY

## "It Wasn't Guts, It Was Insanity"

John DeZurney referred to everyone as his "pal," his trademark greeting to strangers and friends. When he opened a diner in Mahwah, this salutation was an obvious choice as a name for the place.

Following the end of World War II, DeZurney set out to build a career in the diner business. Before the war, he worked at diners in his hometown of Dover. He served in the army, and then after the war he moved to Mahwah with the intention of buying and operating his own diner. Initially, it turned out to be a lunch wagon located on the southbound side of Route 17, adjacent to Moore's Truck Stop. He built a solid relationship with customers, especially truck drivers, who passed the word that Pal's served good coffee and hearty meals. DeZurney's hard work paid off, and in late 1954/early 1955 he opened a larger diner, built by the Manno Dining Car Company, at the same location, near the newly constructed West Ramapo Avenue overpass and jug handle.

DeZurney's decision to open the new Pal's Diner benefitted from good fortune and good timing. It was a period of rapid growth for this northern region of Bergen County. Articles in the 1954 and 1955 editions of the *Ramsey Journal* reported on traffic studies and the expansion of Route 17. This was part of an effort to attract light industry to the area and build shopping centers along the highway.

Manno Dining Car Company matchbook cover. *Courtesy Joe Giannotti.*

But the best development, in terms of boosting DeZurney's business and potential customer base, occurred when the Ford Motor Company relocated its automotive manufacturing operations to Mahwah from Edgewater. Dick Morgan, who worked with John DeZurney off and on for more than twenty years as a dishwasher and short-order cook, said the new diner became a favorite of employees at the Ford plant. Morgan, born in Rome, New York, on April 19, 1928, said he pulled twelve-hour shifts, six days a week and was always entertained by the diner's lively clientele.

Marlene DeZurney Kwak, John's daughter, worked as a waitress and did cash register duty at Pal's during her years as a student at Ramsey High School, from which she graduated in 1957. Marlene's mom, Margaret Johanna, also worked at the diner. Pal's had been up and running prior to the opening of the Ford plant, she recalled. According to an online article at nj.com, July 15, 1955, marked the date when the first car rolled off the Mahwah assembly line. She said Ford's "car carrier" truck drivers were among the diner's most loyal customers.

As for food, Marlene said the diner maintained a basic menu of egg platters, burgers and sandwiches along with daily specials: meatloaf, roast beef, chicken and spaghetti and meatballs. "At lunch time we had customers lined up outside the diner waiting to come in," she said. "We had the grill right behind the counter and people liked that. My dad worked the grill, but he did a bit of everything at the diner. The customers enjoyed talking with him. My dad was a happy-go-lucky guy and generous to a fault. He'd give you the shirt off his back, and he was good to his employees." Some of those employees were his former army buddies who showed up in need of a job.

She said her family's life revolved around the diner business, so it was a sad day when John realized that he needed to sell Pal's in order to care for his wife, who had been ill for many months. In 1974, John sold the business to George Vardoulakis, reportedly for $165,000. Marlene recalled that it was a relatively abrupt decision on the part of her dad. Following that transaction, John briefly became involved with other diner businesses in the Bergen

John DeZurney, 1944. *Courtesy Marlene DeZurney Kwak.*

County towns of Midland Park and Westwood. Margaret Johanna died soon after he sold Pal's, and John passed away in 1981 at the age of sixty-six.

Vardoulakis maintained Pal's, but during the 1980s, business declined due to competition from other area restaurants and diners and the shuttering of the auto plant. Ford's Mahwah plant closed on June 19, 1980, laying off more than 3,700 workers. The Associated Press reported that a two-door, cream-and-tan Fairmont Futura was the last of 6 million vehicles to be completed on the assembly line. By 1992, Vardoulakis wanted to sell the business, but there were no takers in New Jersey.

It was page-one news in the *Grand Rapids Press* when Pal's Diner rolled into the Michigan city at 4:00 a.m. on February 11, 1993, strapped to a tractor trailer. It traveled in two pieces: the main diner body and the front-door vestibule. The arduous journey, more than 1,600 miles, winding along highways and passing through Pennsylvania, Ohio and Michigan, began with a sad farewell in Mahwah on February 3, 1993. Truck drivers and faithful Bergen County customers, including American guitar legend Les Paul, all shed tears as they said farewell.

Michigan restaurant entrepreneurs Barry and Soon Sam Choi Brown managed several eateries in the Grand Rapids area, but they always had a yearning to own a classic Jersey diner. In late 1992, they had learned through business associates that Pal's was on the selling block. They flew to Atlantic City airport, rented a car and drove to Mahwah. Arriving at the diner, Barry and Soon Sam inspected the facility, looked at each other and decided to take the plunge. It was love at first sight, and they made logistical arrangements with state highway authorities and state police to move the popular diner to Grand Rapids.

Looking back at this moment, Barry Brown chuckled during a phone interview in early 2017, confessing that this was an impulsive decision between him and his wife, a bright businesswoman from Canton (Guangzhou), located in China's Guangdong Province. Barry recalled that as the diner was being secured onto the tractor trailer in preparation for the long trek, one Jersey guy patted Barry on the back, admiring him for his courage. "You've got a lot of guts, this guy told me," Barry said. "I told him that it wasn't guts, it was insanity."

Barry confessed that buying the diner may have been a leap of faith, but he also indicated there was one reassuring catalyst that help clinched the decision between him and his wife: a waitress at the diner named Annie Lo Polito. Annie provided a tour of the place for the Michigan couple, pointing out its various flaws and charms. The diner would need considerable work to refurbish it, but if Soon Sam and Barry were willing to embrace the place, the cost would be worth it, she assured them. Barry could see that even though Annie smiled as she spoke, the prospect of Pal's leaving Mahwah was breaking her heart. Still, she wanted to see the diner survive, even if it meant relocating to another state. Barry soon learned that this was more than just sweet affection—Pal's Diner was her salvation.

He recounted Annie's story, which appeared in the October 3, 1996 edition of the *Ridgewood News* and was documented in *The Record*'s February 4, 1993 edition as part of its coverage of the diner leaving Mahwah.

Pal's Diner being prepared for the long haul to Michigan. *Courtesy Marlene DeZurney Kwak.*

Annie had profound emotional ties to the diner. In 1986, Annie, a former beautician, was dropped off at the diner by her husband. "My husband said he'd be back in 45 minutes and never returned," the newspaper quoted her in the article. George Vardoulakis, the owner of the diner, came to her aid by collecting money from his customers and gave her a job as a waitress. After a number of months, the abandoned beautician pulled herself together and became the friendly face of Pal's Diner. "I've been here ever since," she said, quoted in the article. "This diner has been my home."

Inspired by Annie's story, Barry realized that purchasing Pal's was much deeper than just a business transaction. Once it arrived in Grand Rapids, Brown had to put the diner into storage for about three years as he invested $800,000 to repair and upgrade the Jersey gem. He also negotiated to find a suitable location, which turned out to be the Cascade Township East shopping mall. Pal's opened to media fanfare in Grand Rapids on April 10, 1996. He saw a steady uptick in his business over the years. "There are lots of restaurants in Grand Rapids, but a diner is a fun place," Brown said.

Barry kept in touch with Marlene, consulting with her about maintaining the proper arrangement of the interior décor. She said that Brown was very aware of trying to capture the 1950s spirit of a New Jersey diner. Once it was situated in its new location, Marlene and her husband, Nick, visited Pal's in Grand Rapids on two occasions. "Barry and Sam were so excited to see us," Marlene said. "They're the greatest people. They were happy to show us around the diner. Except for a few changes behind the counter, everything was the same." Marlene also said there were no "mixed feelings" about seeing the diner in its new setting. "I was very happy for Barry and Sam and felt happy for the memories that would live on for those who considered the diner a part of their life in New Jersey."

One fan who offered an online testimonial to Pal's is Grand Rapids blogger Tieka Ellis. Tieka and her husband, Eric, visited Pal's on February 28, 2013. "If you're lucky enough to snag the seat across from the soda fountain, you're in the favorite seat of the legendary Les Paul, who ate here quite often when it was in New Jersey," she wrote in her lifestyle blog, *Selective Potential*. "It's literally like you step back into time (the 1950s, that is) when you go inside. Everything is pink. I love this place so much; maybe I can find a cute pink dress."

History does repeat itself in the diner business. Barry once again made news in Grand Rapids by announcing his decision to step down from the diner, much like John DeZurney did more than forty years earlier. An online report in the *Grand Rapids Business Journal*, posted on August 29, 2017, reported that the Browns were "passing the torch" to new ownership. *Grand*

Pal's Diner in Grand Rapids, Michigan. *Courtesy Tieka Ellis, "Selective Potential."*

*Rapids* magazine published an online story on May 18, 2018, stating that the eatery, renamed Dan's Diner, would reopen later that month with an expanded menu and outdoor patio seating.

Barry described his ownership of Pal's as "a complete success story" and noted he was going out on top; business in 2017 was running 25 percent higher than the previous year. Barry and Soon Sam said goodbye to customers and well-wishers on Saturday, October 7, 2017. "My wife and I were the only two people in the place who weren't sad that day. It's time to hand the baton to someone else," he said. "My wife and I have made a good buck in the restaurant business, but it's stressful with long hours. There's lots of hard work involved, and it can be difficult to find good help. We've built a legacy here. Are we sad? No. We're ready to retire. Life changes and this is just another chapter of life." It's also another chapter in the saga of a diner built in New Jersey that operated in Mahwah and then moved to Michigan. Hopefully it's a saga that will continue for the good people of Grand Rapids.

Goodbye, Pal.

# Haircuts on Maple Street

It's a fixture in the community, with a lineage that can be traced back more than 110 years. The Summit Diner, located at 1 Union Place and built by O'Mahony, was installed in 1938. The Summit Historical Society provided a document ("New Jersey Department of Environmental Protection, Office of New Jersey Heritage, Historical Sites Inventory No. 2018; 2610") that spells out basic details on the diner's history, construction date and its appearance: "A classic diner, retaining original features, including sign and Art Deco lettering," with exterior walls of enameled steel and stainless steel trim.

The existence of a lunch wagon in the vicinity of the Union Place/Summit Avenue intersection in this Union County town coincides with the opening of the Summit train station, which was built in 1904–5. The 1905 Summit City Directory lists a "restaurant" by John J. Rooney at 23 Union Place. Given this listing, it suggests that Rooney had established the business in 1904. Subsequent city directories (1909, 1913 and 1916) track the location of Rooney's lunch wagon at 23 Union Place, 75 Union Place and 1 Union Place.

The *Summit Herald*, in its May 17, 1979 issue, published three photos on the history of the Summit Diner, one of which showed Rooney's lunch

Summit Diner. *Photo by M. Gabriele.*

wagon. Rooney moved to Orange in 1920 and there is no listing of a diner or wagon in the next five editions of the city directory, but other newspaper articles, photos and notes from the historical society's files indicate that there was an interim diner or wagon of unknown origin in the vicinity. Beginning in 1930, editions of the city directory list James D. Courakos and Gus Goumas as the owners of a diner at 72 Summit Avenue, which corresponds to the footprint of the current Summit Diner. Records from the historical society cross-referenced the installation of a "new diner building" in 1938 (today's Summit Diner) and listed Goumas and Frank Diakos as the co-owners in 1940.

Goumas, born in Sparta, Greece, operated the diner until his retirement in 1948. He came to the United States in 1913 and was a longtime resident of Summit. He died on February 7, 1971, at the age of seventy-one. Diakos carried on after Goumas stepped away from the business, until he retired in 1965. Born in Molaos, Greece, Diakos arrived in the United States in 1920 and died on March 4, 1995.

Newspaper articles and Summit Historical Society documents indicate that John Greberis and George Contorousis purchased the Summit Diner from Diakos in 1964. According to news accounts, Greberis and Contorousis were friends, born and raised on the Greek island of Andros, and came to America in 1950. One story said that Greberis proudly displayed a ship anchor tattoo on his right forearm, symbolizing his service in the Greek navy and merchant marines. It was during his navy service that he honed his culinary skills.

The two men came to America in search of careers in the New Jersey diner business. Not long after they had arrived in 1950, they worked at a string of diners in East Orange and Freehold. The two men found success in the business, sold those interests and acquired the Summit Diner from Diakos. Contorousis died on May 24, 1998. Jimmy and Michelle Greberis began working at the eatery in 1980 and then became the owners in 1985 after buying out the ownership from John Greberis (Jimmy's uncle) and Contorousis (Michelle's dad).

As A LITTLE BOY growing up in Summit during the 1970s, Eric Evers knew that when the time came for him to get a haircut, it was always two-part process: an iron-clad agreement between him and his father. The first part involved going to Maple Street to get trimmed at Tony's Barber Shop. The second part—Eric's all-important "buy in" for the outing—was breakfast with dad at the Summit Diner.

The father-and-son excursions, ostensibly to keep young Eric well groomed and looking sharp, became more about bonding at the diner and, in the process, created lasting memories. Sitting at the counter and enjoying breakfast with his dad, Eric recalled that he sometimes would feel mildly apprehensive. He imagined that the diner, which bears a resemblance to a train car, would begin moving at any moment, bound for some unknown destination. The concerns were understandable from his youthful perspective, as the diner sits just a short distance from the Summit train station, and Eric could hear and feel an ominous rumble when a train approached.

During his days as a teenager, Eric and his Summit High School buddies shared a fascination with cars and engine mechanics. His prized hot rod was a midnight-blue 1968 Pontiac GTO. He and his friends would park their vehicles on Union Place and stop in at the Summit Diner. It was an idyllic period: cool cars, carefree times, good friends, French fries, hamburgers and sodas. Sadly, in retrospect, after his high school days, Eric decided to sell the GTO.

He joined the Summit Fire Department as a volunteer in 1988. Two years later, he came on board full time. He demonstrated his leadership capabilities as he rose through the ranks as a lieutenant, a battalion chief and deputy chief. On May 26, 2015, he was sworn in as the chief of the Summit Fire Department.

One of the regular duties for the fire department is to do safety inspections at the diner. This involves going into the eatery's crawl space to examine the under-carriage and foundation. The Summit sits on a bed of steel I-beams. After more than eight decades, everything is solid and structurally sound.

Members of the fire department have adopted the Summit Diner as one of their favorite places in town. After fighting a blaze or following late-night shift work, the traditional meal for firemen at the Summit is Taylor Ham and cheese on a roll. Eric said the staff at the diner is most generous to the firefighters. "They open their doors to us, and we appreciate it." Today, when time permits, Eric and his associates grab lunch at the diner. "People around town recognize us as firefighters, so we have plenty to talk about," he said. "Summit has changed a lot over the last thirty years, but the one thing that hasn't changed is the diner. It still looks the same. It's been a constant in the community."

Considering the memories he holds, he was talking about "a constant in the community" as something well beyond the diner's familiar, unchanging appearance. Like other treasured diners throughout the state, the Summit is a gathering place, an everyday station to meet and socialize. The diner's sturdy undercarriage I-beams have supported thousands of get-togethers for families, business colleagues, strangers, lovers and friends.

To paraphrase the lyrics of the 1964 song "Little GTO," recorded by Ronny and the Daytonas, maybe someday Eric will save all his money and buy another midnight-blue GTO. It's easy to picture him motoring along Summit's boulevards on a Saturday morning, waving to friends, enjoying the smooth, seductive purr of the engine and taking a sentimental journey past the barbershop on Maple Street. It's also easy to guess where he's most likely to stop for breakfast.

# Bloomfield Built and Operated for Bloomfield Residents

The Fodero Dining Car Company made its home in Bloomfield and represents the Essex County town's highlight in New Jersey diner history. Joseph P. Fodero started the diner manufacturing business in 1933. Five years later, Fodero and a partner, Milton Glick, relocated the business to

Newark and changed the name of the business to the National Dining Car Company. National suspended its operations during World War II and then returned to Bloomfield, once again under the Fodero name, with a factory at 136 Arlington Avenue. Fodero shuttered its plant in 1981. Joseph Fodero died in June 1989, and his son, Theodore, passed away in February 2012.

Fodero built diners for customers throughout New Jersey and the Northeast, including the heralded hometown eatery known as the State Diner. On April 24, 1954, the State Diner, located at the corner of State and Liberty Streets (adjacent to Bloomfield Avenue), held its grand opening. An article in the April 22, 1954 edition of the *Independent Press* newspaper reported that owners William A. Ramundo, Louis P. Ramundo and Florian M. Walchak touted the eatery, which carried a price tag of $250,000, as "the largest diner in the world, capable of serving 100,000 customers a month." A full-page ad in the same issue of the *Independent Press* declared that the State Diner was "Bloomfield built, Bloomfield operated, for Bloomfield residents."

The story stated that the L-shaped building's 115-foot length and 6,500-square-foot basement space dedicated to food preparation and service qualified it as the world's largest diner. The State employed a staff of forty-four people. Depending on various comparisons, the DeLuxe Diner in Union, which was built by O'Mahony and opened on August 12, 1946, could challenge the State's claim of being world's largest diner. The DeLuxe, also an L-shaped diner, had a length of nearly 134 feet and sixty employees.

Fodero took eight months to build the State Diner—five sections fully equipped with all appliances and cooking stations. "Customers will discover a pleasing décor with comfort [as] the keynote at tables, booths and at the extra-long counter. Lounges also are provided," the *Independent Press* reported. "Waitresses will have light signal systems to save steps. Gas is used throughout as the fuel for heating, air conditioning and all appliances, including ovens, ranges, water heaters, broilers, fryers, dish washers, coffee urns, toasters, steam tables, steam cooker and water chiller, which is the heart of the vibration-free air conditioning system."

By 1958, the State began advertising itself as "Willie's Diner." The name change, perhaps a reference to owner William Ramundo, became official in the 1961 Bloomfield City Directory. A fire on January 13, 1985, forced the diner to temporarily close and remodel. It later changed its name to the State Street Diner. A major fire in the early 2000s caused significant damage. On November 1, 2006, the establishment reopened as the State Street Grill.

Bloomfield's diner history goes back to the early 1900s with the opening of Eriksen's Lunch Wagon, owned and operated by Fred H. Eriksen. The

Eriksen's Lunch Wagon, circa 1924, Bloomfield. *Courtesy Rich Rockwell, Historical Society of Bloomfield.*

lunch wagon business is first listed in the 1910 Bloomfield City Directory. The eatery was located next to Bloomfield National Bank at the intersection of Bloomfield Avenue and Broad Street. A display ad in the August 13, 1915 edition of the *Independent Press and Bloomfield Citizen* mentions F.H. Eriksen's "Business Men's Lunch; Open All Hours of Day and Night."

A second wagon occupied the same spot on Bloomfield Avenue. Still known as Eriksen's Lunch, it was built (circa 1924) by O'Mahony. By about 1930, Eriksen's wagon, as well as the beautiful domed Beaux Arts Bloomfield National Bank building, had been removed and replaced by the high-rise "Frank Leo" building, which stands today in downtown Bloomfield. Frederick Eriksen died on March 14, 1962.

Diner fans in Bloomfield still mourn the loss of their beloved Short-Stop Diner, a Kullman car later modified by Manno. The Short-Stop's first listing in the city directory is 1959. The small diner's signature dish was "eggs in the skillet," as advertised on its billboard roof sign. In the early 2000s, the Short-Stop was converted into a Dunkin' Donuts, which operates today. The basic diner car body remains in place, topped by a brown Dunkin' Donuts roof and orange awnings.

Taqueria Los Güeros, formerly the White Circle System Diner. *Photo by M. Gabriele.*

There was another Short Stop Diner, which was located on Washington Avenue in the nearby town of Belleville. According to information posted on the Diversified Diners website, the Belleville Short Stop was a 1949 "dinette" car (a twelve-foot by twenty-seven-foot frame) built by the Paramount Dining Car Company of Haledon. "Just after World War II, several diner companies offered a dinette style to appeal to returning G.I.'s as a low-cost, easy-entry into the diner business, as an alternative to their much larger sixty-plus seat diners," as stated in a posting by Diversified Diners.

Bloomfield also was home to the White Crescent Diner, a small stainless steel Kullman car located on Broad Street near the corner of Hoover Avenue during the 1950s and 1960s that was later replaced by a brick building simply known as the Crescent Diner. A survivor of Bloomfield's golden diner era is a small 1954 Manno car located on Bloomfield Avenue near Watsessing Avenue. Originally, it was the White Circle System Diner. Today, the structure operates as Taqueria Los Güeros. Other popular current locations in Bloomfield are the Glenwood Family Diner and Restaurant, the Plaza Diner and the Nevada Diner.

# "Its Importance in the Lives of People Who Gathered There"

In sharing his remembrances of Newark's Weequahic Diner, veteran journalist Nat Bodian confessed that he did have a special passion: Nesselrode pie. According to various recipes, the pie, a nearly forgotten confection that was popular in the early twentieth century, contains chestnut puree, cream, alcohol (usually rum or a fruit liqueur), raisins, currants and shaved dark chocolate.

"I fondly recall my visits to the Weequahic Diner in the post–World War II years, usually after Saturday night dates and later as a young newlywed," Bodian wrote in his online journal, *Old Newark*. "Whenever we went to a show, concert, or any social event, we'd often wind up the night with a stop at the Weequahic Diner for 'coffee and.' I had a passion for the diner's Nesselrode pie. During the wait to get in—and there was always a wait—we would meet friends, neighbors, former schoolmates, perhaps our doctor or dentist; people we knew and with whom we could chat. It seemed to me at that time that the warm friendly atmosphere around the diner made it as much of an attraction as its good food."

Nat Bodian died on May 1, 2010, at the age of eighty-nine. He began his career as a young reporter in the late 1930s and said that the Weequahic Diner was a landmark "that had become the heart and soul of Newark's bustling and upwardly mobile Jewish community. It occupied a triangular strip of land at 306–308 Elizabeth Avenue bounded by Hawthorne Avenue on the south and East Peddie Street on the north."

Kullman built the Weequahic Diner, which opened in 1938. Harold Kullman, a 1941 graduate of Weequahic High School and the eventual second-generation leader of the diner builder, said "at the time it was one of the largest diners we had built. Everyone from the neighborhood went there." Kullman, interviewed in 2015, said he ate at the Weequahic with his high school buddies at least once a week. Stuffed cabbage, meat loaf, brisket of beef and potato pancakes were his favorite dishes. Harold Kullman passed away on March 19, 2018.

Leo Bauman owned the Weequahic Diner and had established himself as a Newark restaurateur. The Colonial Grill, located at 437 Broadway and listed in the 1934 Newark City Directory, was Bauman's first establishment. Not long after the Weequahic Diner opened, Bauman's brother Morris fled Europe, came to New Jersey and worked as a partner with Leo. Writer Paula Borenstein, a 1967 graduate of Weequahic High School and the co-founder of the Elizabeth Arts Council, shared transcripts of her February 2007 interview with Louise Bauman, the wife of Morris Bauman. Louise, born in Vienna, Austria, on August 4, 1912, said that she and Morris came to Newark in 1938. Morris joined his brother working at the diner, acclimating himself to his new city and the demanding pace of the diner business. "He [Morris] didn't know the language so he helped in the kitchen," Louise recalled.

Louise also divulged her harrowing experiences navigating through Europe during the dark days of the mid-1930s. She met Morris at a café in Vienna, and they married in 1935. Due to the growing Nazi threat, they were frantic to leave Europe

Leo Bauman. *Courtesy Jewish Historical Society of New Jersey, Whippany.*

and come to America, but they had to deal with numerous complications. "We couldn't get out together, because you had to leave on a quota system, and the quota system was [based on] where you were born. I was born in Vienna. Morris was on another quota. He was born in Poland. But at that time England opened up a camp for young Jewish men that had papers, and that in the future they will be able to leave for America. My husband had papers, so he was able to [go to] the camp in England.

Members of the online Weequahic High School alumni group shared their remembrances of the diner via e-mail. Leo Bauman's colorful, outspoken personality emerged as the most vivid memory among the Weequahic faithful. Teenagers would sit and socialize after finishing their meals, but Leo was more interested in keeping the line moving and seating other customers. Perry Hamburg, a former Hillside resident and a regular patron in the 1940s, said he found Leo Bauman to be as "entertaining and enjoyable as the great food, service and ambiance." To speed up customer turnover, Hamburg said Leo would announce over the diner's public address system, "'Ladies and gentlemen, lots of people are waiting outside, but don't let that bother you. Finish your meal whenever you're ready.' And then, after five seconds of silence, Leo shouted: 'Now get ready!'"

The Weequahic's salad, bowl of pickles and cheesecake are recognized by fans as the signature classics of the diner. Two online articles (from myveronanj.com and nj.com) identify a Danish pastry chef named Lars

Jensen as the cheesecake creator, with the recipe coming from Lindy's Restaurant in New York City. Denberg's Bakery, located near the diner, supplied the diner with fresh bread, cake, rolls and other baked goods. An online posting of an original copy of a Weequahic menu had a paper-clipped, typed page with special selections for Sunday dinner, which included main course, soup, appetizer, dessert and a beverage. All the meals were $1.50 or less. The choices were fish platters (fried fillet of lemon sole, baked bluefish, Maryland soft-shell crab, broiled Spanish mackerel and broiled lake trout) and roasts (prime rib, baked Virginia ham, Jersey loin of pork, Long Island duckling and breaded veal cutlet).

Larry Rozolsky said his mom, Sonja (known as "Sunny"), worked as the head waitress and night manager at the diner during the 1950s and 1960s. Rozolsky, a 1962 graduate of Union High School, said his mom put him to work as a bus boy and dishwasher. "I wore a shirt, suit and tie as a bus boy and then changed my clothes to wash dishes."

The diner's long counter became a designated "neutral ground" for the denizens of Newark's late-night scene, with prostitutes, vice squad officers and reputed mobsters all sitting side by side—enjoying their meals during an unspoken, temporary truce. This was the "3:00 a.m. crowd," according to Rozolsky. "They all knew each other. That's the way it was back in those days."

Rock-and-roll legends Frankie Valli and the Four Seasons were among the noteworthy nighttime customers at the diner during the late 1950s. The diner served as an after-hours pit stop for the quartet following performances at nearby lounges and nightclubs, Rozolsky said. "Before they were famous as the Four Seasons, my mom told me they would come to the diner late at night after a show and sit in one of the corner tables. She brought them coffee and dinner rolls."

"Morris and Leo were very gracious to the customers," he continued. "They were characters, but people loved them. Customers were always treated with respect, no matter who they were. The history, warmth and friendliness that the Bauman brothers created lives on within the people that had the great fortune to eat or work at the diner."

Menu cover, Weequahic Diner. *Courtesy Jewish Historical Society of New Jersey.*

*Parade* magazine, in its March 11, 1945 edition, published a portrait of a waitress named Stella Cuttic, who had the "great fortune" to work at the Weequahic Diner. The article was a window into the life of a young waitress and the diner environment as World War II was drawing to a close, describing her as "a smart, little waitress who piles up tips that more than triple her salary." The story said she arrived at the diner at 10:30 a.m. to eat a "leisurely breakfast" of orange juice, ham, eggs, toast and coffee before starting work at 11:00 a.m. Her shift ended at 8:00 p.m.

> *Stella, who works in the Weequahic Diner in Newark, New Jersey, knows her job and knows people. There is a brisk demand for her services, and she is well aware of the value of her work to her employer and her customers. Stella's success as a waitress is attributable to her slightly aloof, quiet air of confidence. For the past three years—since leaving her home in a small Pennsylvania coal mining town at the age of sixteen to earn her own living—Stella has been a waitress. "I like the work," says Stella, "because there are new people to see every day, and it's fun to listen to their conversations. Women always talk about men, and men always talk about business."*

As a distinct Newark neighborhood, Weequahic began to coalesce in the early years of the twentieth century. *Weequahic*, a Leni-Lenape word, is translated as "head of the cove." A business ad in the pages of the January 1914 *Newark Call* newspaper beckoned potential home buyers and investors to consider opportunities in the "Weequahic Tract. Large profits will be made in real estate in this locality within the next few years." Pulitzer Prize–winning novelist Philip Roth (1933–2018), a 1950 Weequahic High School graduate, made reference to the diner in his 1969 novel *Portnoy's Complaint*. The *New York Times*, in its February 28, 1969 edition, reported that the Weequahic enclave "provided the focus" for Roth's popular novel.

Long-simmering racial strife in Newark reached a boiling point when an uprising began on the night of July 12, 1967. A special report posted July 12, 2017, by nj.com, marking the fiftieth anniversary of the tragic episode, wrote that Governor Richard Hughes met with black community leaders on July 16, 1967. "Both sides wanted the riots to end, so they reached an agreement. Newarkers were left to clean up the pieces of a broken city." Twenty-six people died, and hundreds were injured.

The final days of the Weequahic Diner played out as the 1960s drew to a close. Phil Yourish, Weequahic High School class of 1964, became a teacher in the Newark Public School System and recalled dining at the Weequahic during the late 1960s. The Weequahic Diner appears in the 1974 Newark City Directory, but no owner is listed. There's no listing for the diner in the 1976 city directory.

While they ran the Weequahic Diner, Leo and Morris Bauman decided to diversify with the Claremont Diner in Verona, which opened on May 26, 1955. A twenty-four-hour operation, the diner had a seating capacity of two hundred and housed a bakery. An advertising flyer for the Claremont, from "your hosts Leo and Morris Bauman," highlighted "New Jersey's most beautiful patio dining room" at the diner. The diner suffered a kitchen fire just three days after its grand opening, but the damage was contained and the Claremont reopened a week later.

A feature in the June 22, 1969 *Newark Sunday News* ("Table Talk") gave a glowing review of the Claremont Diner:

> *If the Claremont Diner is indeed a diner, then it has got to be one of the most elegant ones in this man's world. True, it has the external trappings of that hurry-up convenience that one encounters in town and on the highway alike. There is the usual counter with stools and booths up front, but when you have passed all this you move into a different culinary world altogether. Beyond are three rooms that combine three different decorating styles for a setting that can challenge the finest of restaurants. A dinner buffet is served Mondays and Thursdays at $6.50 with prime ribs, stuffed lobster thermidor, [shrimp] scampi, tenderloin tidbits, potato pancakes, noodle pudding, miniature stuffed cabbage rolls, Swedish meatballs, cold crab, fish in aspic and a host of other dishes plus a sweets table.*

The review ended with this sentence: "The Weequahic Diner is still a successful and respected part of the [Bauman] operation." Leo Bauman died on February 8, 1960, at the age of fifty-eight. Morris Bauman succumbed on August 26, 1973. He was sixty-five.

Another organization purchased the Claremont Diner business from the Bauman family in 1974. The *Verona-Cedar Grove Times* reported that a fire on September 8, 1976, gutted the diner. By the summer of 1977, it had been rebuilt as a modern, palatial structure, but there was a second fire on September 30, 1980.

Another Clairmont Diner (note the different spelling of the name) opened on Route 3 in Clifton, on the site of the old Aztec Diner, in the early 1990s, but by 1999, the eatery had closed, replaced by a car dealership that opened in June 2001. The HBO TV series *The Sopranos* chose Clifton's Clairmont as a location shoot in episode fourteen of the show's second season, which aired on January 16, 2000.

Weequahic High School classmates continue to share stories about how the diner became a landmark in their lives. Enid Kesselman Gort, PhD, class of 1957, in an e-mail, described herself as

> *a habitué of the Weequahic Diner during my later high school and college years. Much of my social life centered around the diner and it was there that I met my first husband, who would come for a late dinner after closing his liquor store. At the time, I was vaguely aware of the role played by the diner in cementing relationships within the community. Years later, after becoming a cultural anthropologist, I regretted not having had the theoretical and methodological skills that would have enabled me to take a more analytical approach to my surroundings. That being said, I think I still have a feel for the place and its importance in the lives of people of all ages who gathered there.*

# "Nothing Helps Scenery Like Ham and Eggs"

Three diners in New Jersey are named in honor of the great American writer Mark Twain (Samuel Langhorne Clemens): the Huck Finn Diner and the Mark Twain Diner and Restaurant, both in Union, and the Tom Sawyer Diner in Paramus. The Mark Twain Diner first opened in 1967. The current Mark Twain is a Kullman car installed in 1983, followed by several expansions and renovations. The Huck Finn, also a Kullman diner, originally opened in 1963 as the Peter Pan Diner. After the diner remodeled and expanded in 1991, the name changed to Huck Finn.

A three-alarm blaze on September 12, 2006, destroyed the Tom Sawyer Diner. An online post reported that the original diner opened in 1974. A spokeswoman for the diner said the demand from loyal customers inspired the effort to rebuild. "Our customers wanted us back, and we wanted to come back and be part of the community." The diner was rebuilt and reopened on March 4, 2008.

According to information posted on the website Twain Quotes, Mark Twain (1835–1910) gave at least sixteen lectures in the Garden State from 1869 to 1907, entertaining audiences in Newark, Trenton, Paterson, Jersey

*Above*: Mark Twain Diner. *Photo by M. Gabriele.*

*Left*: Mark Twain portrait, 1907. *Courtesy Library of Congress.*

City, Princeton and other towns. What was his opinion of the Garden State? Barbara Schmidt, Mark Twain archivist and publisher of Twain Quotes, in a July 31, 2017 e-mail note, wrote that Twain apparently "didn't think too highly of New Jersey," at least in the early years of his career. Based on her study of his writings, she said Twain considered the state to be "a backwater" compared to the more glamorous cultural offerings of New York City.

Schmidt cited a passage from Twain's book *The Innocents Abroad*, published in 1869, in which he mockingly wrote about the "old connoisseurs from the wilds of New Jersey who laboriously learn the difference between a fresco and a fire-plug, and from that day forward feel privileged to void their critical *bathos* on painting, sculpture, and architecture forever more." ("Bathos" is defined as the act of a writer or a poet falling into trite, inconsequential and absurd metaphors and descriptions.) Schmidt did write that "over the years, he came to have a number of friends (influential and wealthy individuals) who lived in New Jersey, and his attitudes likely changed." Twain came to Nutley in December 1893 to see his chum H.C. Bunner, the editor of *Puck Magazine*—a meeting between the two accomplished literary figures documented by a short article in the December 11, 1893 edition of the *New York Times*.

In his book *Roughing It*, a semi-fictional collection of his wanderings in the West, published in 1872, Twain expressed diner-like food sensibilities, rambling on about his fondness for fried bacon, black coffee, hot bread and molasses while enjoying the outdoors of the Nevada Territory. He described the book as "a personal narrative…a record of several years of variegated vagabondizing":

> And it was comfort in those succeeding days to sit up and contemplate the majestic panorama of mountains and valleys spread out below us and eat ham and hard boiled eggs, while our spiritual natures reveled alternately in rainbows, thunderstorms, and peerless sunsets. Nothing helps scenery like ham and eggs.

## "My Mother's Heart Was Broken"

This is a story that involves two entrepreneurs from Greece, two European businessmen, a young man and woman from Poland, legendary fluffy pancakes made by a German cook, a minor-league baseball player named

Eddie and a diner that operated in two New Jersey towns before being shipped off to Germany.

If nothing else, this tale demonstrates that classic, factory-built diners were designed to be portable structures. They were a movable commodity that could be bought or sold, rebuilt or renovated and relocated to have a new life in a new town, state or country. It also meant that during the twentieth century, being portable provided financial advantages to diner owners. By definition, they weren't fixed structures—they were taxed like a piece of equipment rather than as a permanent building. The only catch was that the diner owner typically didn't own the property on which the diner sat, which meant land leases might expire or landlords and rents could change. A spokesman from the Jerry O'Mahony Company quoted in a September 23, 1951 *New York Times* article explained the advantages of a diner's portability, saying that a diner "is erected in a plant, moved to a site and placed on a foundation from which it can be moved at any time desired. Because it is movable, it is classified as personal property and not real estate, and is taxed as such."

The ballad of the Teamsters Diner begins in Haldedon in the 1940s, when Paramount built a diner for a successful Red Bank businessman named William "Bill" Noglows. As detailed in an article in the August 29, 2003 edition of *The Hub* newspaper, Noglows arrived in America as a seventeen-year-old immigrant from Greece. The third volume of the book *History of Monmouth County New Jersey, 1664–1920*, noted that Noglows was born in Greece on December 1, 1893, and traveled to the United States in 1910. He came to Red Bank in 1911, "straining every nerve to gain a little headway, denying himself every pleasure in order to save money to make an independent start in business." The ambitious young man established himself by operating a peanut cart at the corner of Broad and Front Streets. Soon he owned three carts and in 1912 demonstrated his streetwise business instincts by opening a shoe shine parlor, which was followed by the Red Bank Candy Kitchen and three different restaurants and luncheonettes. Noglows enlisted in the army in 1917 and, one year later, became a U.S. citizen.

In 1945, Noglows ordered a diner from Paramount and christened it the Monmouth Diner, which was located at 65 Monmouth Street at the corner of Drummond Place. John Morris, who also came from Greece, was Noglows's partner at the Monmouth Diner. The 1956 Red Bank City Directory includes the Monmouth Diner as a business, but the 1958–59 directory lists its address on Monmouth Street as "vacant."

Mounmouth Diner, Red Bank. *Courtesy George Severini, Dorn's Classic Images.*

A contract dated June 26, 1959, stated that diner builder Manno had acquired the Monmouth Diner and sold it to the brothers Edward and Anthony Karpilo. The sale price was $14,595 for the diner, listed in "as is" condition. The contract indicated that the diner's dimensions were forty-five feet long by sixteen feet wide, plus a vestibule, with seven booths and twenty-one counter stools. Karpilo placed his eatery at the corner of Fairfield Road and Hollywood Avenue in Fairfield, near the Curtiss-Wright aerospace plant located on Fairfield Road and close to the Route 46/Hollywood Avenue interchange. He accurately reasoned that this spot would attract hungry truck drivers and factory workers. He named his place the Teamsters Diner in honor of the many truckers and Teamsters Union members who were regular customers.

Not long after the diner opened its doors, Eddie Karpilo became a Fairfield personality, famous for his many sports stories that entertained customers. By 1980, Eddie had bought out his brother and became the sole proprietor of the diner. In April 1986, Teamsters Diner gained attention when it became a location for the shooting of a scene in the movie *Angel Heart*, a psychological suspense/thriller directed by Alan Parker and starring Robert De Niro, Mickey Rourke and Lisa Bonet, which was released in 1987.

The mid-1980s also saw the arrival of two employees at Teamsters Diner: Margaret Jacek and Peter Przygodzki. Both emigrated from Poland, although they didn't know each other prior to moving to New Jersey. Margaret arrived in 1985 and grew up on a farm outside Krakow. Peter lived in the city of Slupsk, not far from the coast of the Baltic Sea, and came to New Jersey in 1987. They landed at the Teamsters Diner separately through respective family connections associated with Eddie Karpilo.

Margaret and Peter spoke little English when they first came to New Jersey and were thankful to get jobs at the diner. "Peter washed dishes, did cleaning and maintenance, and I was a waitress and a short-order cook," Margaret said, interviewed in January 2018. She woke up at 4:00 a.m. and was the first person to arrive at the diner, making coffee and heating the grill. "Eddie was the life of the diner," Margaret said. "We had a lot of business people, policemen, town workers and politicians come to the diner for lunch. They used to say that there was more business conducted at the diner than at Fairfield town hall."

George Rosewall, a Teamsters Diner regular, said Karpilo was a good storyteller. Rosewall said Karpilo regaled customers with tales from his navy days and his short-lived baseball career. Karpilo served in the navy during World War II and played one season of minor-league baseball in 1948 for two teams in the Border League. Injuries derailed his baseball career. Rosewall, who worked as a contractor in the building trades, had an early morning breakfast routine of meeting his dad, Roger, and his business partners at the Teamsters Diner.

Margaret said there was a cheerful family atmosphere at the diner. "For me it was like a family, because I had no family here. The American people helped me learn the language. The people at the diner were very kind to me. Americans are very welcoming people." At this point in the conversation, Margaret became wistful. She grew up on a family farm in Poland, growing potatoes, wheat and sweet beets and raising cattle, pigs and horses. Farm life involved rigorous manual work. "My mom [Maria] told me to leave the farm and go to the United States for a better life." Margaret said that, even though she understood the wisdom behind her mother's advice, it was a sad, difficult separation for her. Initially, after coming to the United States, Margaret lived with an uncle and aunt in Caldwell. "I had three brothers, but I was the only daughter. I think my mother's heart was broken when I left, even though she encouraged me to go. It's very hard when you're an immigrant. America becomes your country, but my heart was always in Poland."

Teamsters Diner, Fairfield. *Courtesy Peter Lundell.*

Aside from Eddie, the other star personality at the diner was a German chef named Horst Pruffer, who worked at Teamsters for more than twenty years and was famous for his light, fluffy, high-rise pancakes. Margaret said Horst had his own secret pancake recipe. His other specialties of the house were meatloaf, chili, chicken parmigiana and homemade soups.

Peter and Margaret bonded and developed a romantic relationship. They married on September 14, 1991. One year later, they bought the Teamsters Diner from Eddie. "He said he was finished owning the diner and sold it to us. He was our mentor. He was always at the diner to talk with customers, even after he sold it." Edward J. Karpilo died on January 10, 1998, at the age of seventy-three.

By 1999, Margaret and Peter realized that it was time for them to sell the diner, mainly due to the rising costs for leasing the property on which the diner sat, but there were few serious offers. One day, two German businessmen, Thomas Wolf and Thomas Matszok, showed up at the diner, hoping to buy the place. According to newspaper reports, there were several months of negotiations, which concluded with a sale price of $48,000. Logistics were arranged for moving the diner, and the Teamsters Diner closed its doors in Fairfield for the last time on Friday, January 28, 2000. On that afternoon, a reporter from a local newspaper quoted Margaret, who confessed that she felt "an aura of sadness, but I can't let people see it. So many people came in today to say goodbye. It was hard for me to look at some of the faces."

Removal of the diner took place February 2–3, 2000. It was loaded onto a ship in Port Elizabeth and began its journey to Karlsruhe, German, where it operates today as the American Diner Durlach. The diner's website invites customers to "travel back to the time of Rock and Roll with us and the iconic lifestyle of the 1950s. In a lovingly restored, original 1950s diner you can enjoy stylish real American cuisine in Durlach. Discover our wide selection of beef and chicken; burgers freshly prepared for you on the grill. We also offer homemade chili, chicken wings, hot dogs, crunchy salads, fine milkshakes and original American beer and soft drink specialties. Enjoy the American way of life and the best burger in town."

Margaret's final sorrow of her Teamsters Diner experience came when, talking through tears, she remembered her husband, Peter, who died on January 20, 2016, at the age of forty-seven. "He was a wonderful man."

# You Just Keep Me Hanging On

Musician Pete Bremy was in good spirits four days before his sixty-fifth birthday, on a Wednesday morning in October 2017. He enjoyed brunch at his favorite place, the Roxbury Diner. Bremy is a bass player with a rock résumé that includes his many years of recordings and tours with Vanilla Fudge, Cactus and other bands. "I've been to a lot of diners over the years," he said, wearing his trademark shades and cap. "I've lived in New Jersey all my life [originally from Paterson], and being a musician, I'm a late-night person and I eat out late often."

He and his wife, Beverly Simon Bremy, sometimes portray themselves as the "Dineramic Duo" and post their diner adventures on Facebook. He ranks the Roxbury Diner as his favorite, based on the diner's friendly service and proximity to his home, the consistently good coffee and the quality of his two go-to diner meals: eggs over easy with bacon and a cheeseburger.

In August 1967, Bremy went to a concert in Pleasureland Park in Oakland to see a band called Vanilla Fudge. "It was the first time I heard the song 'You Keep Me Hanging On.' It was the day before their first album was released. They weren't famous yet. It was their live performance that blew me away, not the record."

*Left*: Pete Bremy at the Roxbury Diner. *Photo by M. Gabriele.*

*Below*: Bendix Diner. *Photo by M. Gabriele.*

After the concert, he became a fan of the quartet (Carmine Appice, Tim Bogert, Mark Stein and Vince Martell). Bremy and his best friend, Jeff Guenther, another Vanilla Fudge fan, decided to see the band perform at the Fillmore East in New York City on March 8, 1969. At the time, Bremy and Guenther were living in Wayne, and Guenther was celebrating a birthday. The two Jersey teens attended the late show. By the time they started driving home, it was sunrise, and in the early morning haze of their adventure, they suddenly realized they were quite hungry. So, they stopped for breakfast at the Bendix Diner.

Fast-forward thirty years, and Bremy was an aspiring, hardworking professional musician, performing regularly in New Jersey clubs. Networking through his musical associates, he was introduced to Vanilla Fudge guitarist Vince Martell, and they became friends. In February 1999, Martell invited Bremy to attend his performance at the Crow's Nest in Hackensack. After the show closed, Bremy, Martell and friends wanted to get a bite to eat in the early morning hours. Someone suggested the nearby Bendix Diner "because it stays open all night." Master Diners of Pequannock built the Bendix, circa 1947.

It was thirty years between cups of coffee for Bremy at the Bendix, and no visits in between. The serendipity of the moment made him smile. "The first time I went to the Bendix as a teenager, I was a fan of the Vanilla Fudge. And then, thirty years later, I walked into the diner with a member of the Vanilla Fudge."

Good fortune followed Bremy after that second stop at the Bendix, and he remained in touch with Martell. Three years later, the Vanilla Fudge asked Bremy to fill in for bassist Tim Bogert just prior to the band's extended tour of the United States and Europe. Bremy has remained affiliated with the band ever since. Feeling sentimental several years ago, Bremy took Beverly to the Bendix Diner and told her about his Vanilla Fudge story. "They were and are my favorite band, and I'm now a member."

# Family Roots in Nafpaktos

The Florham Park Diner celebrated its twenty-fifth year of business in August 2016, but the silver anniversary is just one chapter of the family-owned eatery. Vicki Grapsas—the gracious owner, partner and diner entrepreneur—said that the family's American story begins in the 1920s, when her great-grandfather Demetrios Papaharalambous, whom she never met, left Greece and landed in Chicago, where he began working at and then owning restaurants and diners.

George Grapsas came to the United States in 1968 to work for Demetrios, his grandfather. George (Vicki's dad) grew up in Nafpaktos, a port town in western Greece known for its medieval history. George had served in the Greek army's Special Forces and decided to pursue a career in Chicago. He learned the restaurant business from the bottom up, first working as a busboy and a waiter. After two years, George relocated to New Jersey and began working at diners that had family connections to his Greek roots. He soon became a skillful cook and gained the necessary financial and managerial insights on how to run a diner business. In 1975, he purchased the Hamilton, a diner in Morristown, and ran it with his wife, Ginette, who came to America from Quebec, Canada. The couple later purchased a seafood restaurant in Newton and opened a steakhouse franchise in Florham Park.

Deciding to downsize and consolidate their efforts, George and Ginette sold these aforementioned businesses and, in 1991, bought the Park Place Luncheonette, a storefront property in a cluster of businesses adjacent to the Columbia Turnpike, which they developed into the Florham Park Diner through two major expansions and renovations in 2002 and 2004.

Vicki worked as a waitress and a hostess during her high school and college years. She graduated from New York University in 2004 with a business major and worked almost ten years in the fashion industry but decided to join her parents and brother, Demetri, in 2013 to manage the diner. Having grown up in the business, she takes pride in maintaining the traditions and spirit of the family enterprise.

Vicki Grapsas, Florham Park Diner.
*Photo by M. Gabriele.*

# Diner Joe and Good Times in East Newark

Joe Baum, a son of East Newark, lived on Grant Avenue from the mid-1930s to the late 1950s. Joe's parents owned the building, which included apartments for an assortment of aunts and uncles. In 1936, as a teenager, he got a job at Harrison Supply, a masonry materials and concrete plant perched along the Passaic River, and eventually became a crane operator. Joe and his buddies enjoyed ten-cent glasses of beer at a neighborhood tavern named Murphy's.

Linda Buset and Joe Baum. *Photo by M. Gabriele.*

These were good times, and Joe took pride in his well-connected neighborhood. Everything he needed was in walking distance. And nearly every morning on his way to work, he would stop for a ham (or bacon) and egg breakfast at a place called Tops Grill on Passaic Avenue—an early iteration of today's Tops Diner. Joe said that Tops was small and friendly, never too busy, with good food, coffee and daily soups. Eating at Tops started his lifelong love affair with diners.

In 1943, Joe enlisted in the army and served in Europe during World War II. He came home in 1946, and as soon as he got off the boat, he married his sweetheart, Anna Videyko, from nearby Harrison. He returned to work at Harrison Supply and restarted his morning routine of breakfast at Tops.

Joe and his family moved to Nutley in 1958, but he continued to eat at Tops and other diners in the area. "When I was a little girl, my father used to drag me along with him to his favorite diners," Linda Buset, Joe's daughter, said. "What I remember most is that, at all the diners we visited, my dad knew everyone. He loves to talk. People would come up to us and say hello. He's 'Diner Joe.'"

Linda, a 1969 graduate of Nutley High School, and Joe, who turned ninety-eight years old on February 17, 2019, frequented their hometown Nutley Diner to continue their daughter-and-father lunch outings. When Joe and Anna celebrated their seventieth wedding anniversary on June 8, 2016, the family gathered at the Nutley Diner for a feast. Diner Joe was in his glory. "We had the party at the diner; where else?" Linda said.

THE 1938 EAST NEWARK City Director has a listing for Tops Grill at 500 Passaic Avenue (the same location as today's Tops Diner), owned by Jess P. Persson. This suggests the diner opened in the mid-1930s; there's no mention of the diner in the 1929 city directory. It's also possible that Persson ran a lunch wagon at or near the Passaic Avenue location prior to opening the diner. His obituary in the December 27, 1946 edition of the *Jersey Journal* described him as the "owner of a lunch wagon in East Newark." Persson was born on October 7, 1884, in Jersey City and died on December 26, 1946.

News items by nj.com and an article in the August 28, 2003 edition of the *Jersey Journal* tracked the evolution of Tops. The *Journal* article reported that George Golemis came to the United States from Greece as a teenager in 1968 and began working at restaurants and diners in New York City. The Golemis family purchased the diner in 1972 and has overseen major expansions and remodeling projects—in 1989 and 2004. Tops sits as a regal blue-and-silver landmark adjacent to the Clay Street Bridge. Thrillist, the food, travel and entertainment website, in 2018 selected East Newark's Tops Diner for its list of "the twenty-one best diners in America." *Time Out* magazine, in 2017, rated Tops Diner as the best diner in America. These honors have translated into national acclaim for the diner. Cars with license plates from throughout the country can be seen in the diner's parking lot on any day of the week.

Tops Diner. *Photo by M. Gabriele.*

Reviewers and food critics rave about the diner's baked goods, seafood, meatloaf and steaks. (This author enjoyed eggs Benedict for lunch on New Year's Day 2019. The diner's strawberry cheesecake is a slice of heaven.) There's a full bar for cocktails and a small diner counter.

The food is exceptional, but it's the service that sets Tops apart from most diners. The place is habitually packed, yet the efficient wait staff knows how to take care of business. A legion of highly synchronized, good-natured women and men, dressed in black Tops uniform shirts, dart throughout the diner to deliver orders and respond to special requests from customers. Engrossed by these frenetic maneuvers while eating my eggs Benedict, I recalled John Baeder's words in the introduction chapter of this book regarding the invisible choreography that he called the "diner dance." I realized I was surrounded by the magic of the dance, just as he described it—a eureka moment on the first day of the New Year.

IT WAS A SAD day in the Essex County township of Nutley when Joseph M. Baum passed away on the evening of March 26, 2019, just one month after his ninety-eighth birthday. His daughter, Linda, Joe's faithful and favorite diner companion, was at his side. Joe was part of the "Greatest Generation," the generation that lived through the Great Depression, won World War II and put diners on the map. Along with family and friends, diners were a big part of his life. It was a good life.

"He was a storyteller," Linda wrote in an essay as a requiem for her dad. As mentioned, she said he loved to talk. It was this gift of gab that made him popular with acquaintances at diner counters. "Whether they were stories about his work years at Harrison Supply or his time in Germany during World War II, he told his stories to anyone who would listen. Joe was a generous man. He was a hard worker, a dreamer, a gentleman and a man of compassion."

Farewell, Diner Joe. Thanks for the memories.

## Back to the Drawing Board

After more than sixty-five years in the business, there's still creativity coming from Herb Enyard's drawing board—an old-school drawing board, that is; no computer screens or Internet connections. One of his most recent creations is the stainless steel and glass vestibule that adorns Paul's Diner, located on Route 46 in Mountain Lakes, which was completed in June 2017. Enyard and his son, Edward, collaborated on that project.

New Jersey diners designed and built by Enyard and his company PMC Diners Inc. include the Wayne Hills Diner on the Hamburg Turnpike in Wayne, the Stafford Diner on Route 72 in Manahawkin, the State Line Diner on Route 17 in Mahwah, the Pompton Queen on Route 23 in Pompton Plains and Legends Diner on County Avenue in Secaucus. Diners designed by Enyard outside the state include the landmark Eveready Diner on Route 9 in Hyde Park, New York, which opened in the fall of 1995, and Mike's Olympic Grill Diner in the Elm Park section of Staten Island, which debuted in September 2007. He noted that the Olympic Grill, which features an intricate stone façade and large picture windows, was the last "complete" modular, prefabricated diner that he produced at his Oakland facility.

The Eveready Diner—with its signature tower, distinctive interior accented with decorative hanging ceiling lights and a dazzling mirrored/ stainless steel counter—was built in Oakland and transported to the site in Hyde Park. Enyard said that the Eveready project began with original

Eveready Diner, Hyde Park, New York. *Photo by M. Gabriele.*

drawings and design concepts by Morris Nathanson of Pawtucket, Rhode Island. PMC made changes to Nathanson's designs as the manufacturing process unfolded. Nathanson, the founder of Morris Nathanson Design (but now retired), is a world-famous designer and artist. He and his company also did design work on the imaginative Skylark Diner located on Route 1 in Edison, which opened in 2006.

A press statement issued when the Eveready Diner was delivered twenty-four years ago, provided by Enyard, said that tractor trailer trucks transported the structure in eight sections, with a police escort, from Oakland to the location in Hyde Park that previously was the site of the Town and Country Diner, which was demolished in March 1995. The first sections of the Eveready arrived on May 4, 1995. The diner had a price tag of $1 million. "Herb Enyard is proud to point out that his company has no assembly line. His staff of about fifteen people design and custom-build diners. They buy some items like stool shafts and ovens, but everything else is made by hand."

Karen Maserjian Shan, an account manager with IMPACT PR and Communications Ltd., interviewed Eveready owner Gus Serroukas in 2015 for the *Poughkeepsie Journal*, when she worked as a freelance writer for the newspaper. Serroukas had just won the Dutchess County Economic Development Corporation's 2015 Business Excellence Award. She wrote that Serroukas, a native of Greece, opened the Double O Doughnut Luncheonette in Poughkeepsie in 1968. "I had a nice coffee shop," Serroukas said, quoted in the story. "I became very busy. I [took] care of my customers. The people, they liked me."

Serroukas starts his day by sitting at the Eveready counter for breakfast, drinking multiple cups of decaf coffee and talking with his customers and employees, according to Suzanne Liguori, who has worked as a waitress at the diner for the last thirteen years. Suzanne most appreciates the relationships she's formed with her regular customers, many of whom are senior citizens. "I love working at the diner. It is a business and a busy place, but I have fun with my regulars. This is their 'out' for the day and they enjoy themselves. Sometimes I feel like I'm an entertainer. They bring me Christmas presents and flowers. I get kisses and hugs. They bring their families to meet me."

She seemed tickled by the notion that the Eveready is a Jersey diner that just happens to be located in Hyde Park. "Someday I'll have to go to a Jersey diner in New Jersey."

Customer traffic at the Eveready includes students from nearby Marist College, visitors to the Home of Franklin D. Roosevelt National Historic Site and autumn foliage tourists. "People are in awe of the place when they first walk in," she said, referring to the diner's stunning architecture. There is another Eveready Diner in Brewster, New York, with a completely different architectural design, which has ownership connections with the Serroukas family.

Born in Paterson in 1934, Enyard is the last of the Garden State's golden age diner builders. He began his career at Silk City in 1952 and then moved on to Paramount in the early 1960s. He became president of Paramount in 1970 and then recast the business as PMC in Oakland.

Enyard estimated that he's designed and built more than three hundred diners during his career. As a designer, his primary concern is a diner's commercial success and that the structure functions to customer specifications. "You have to consider mobility, safety and flow [of people and food] inside the diner. You learn a lot from your customers, especially when it comes to things like designing a kitchen layout." He's also aware of the cultural significance of diners and his contributions to the tradition. "Diners are an American achievement." He remains active as a consultant, primarily on diner redesigns. Enyard said that he and his wife, Gilda, enjoy an occasional road trip, "visiting the diners that I've built."

# Family Owned and Operated

The intersection of Millburn and Morris Avenues in Springfield in the early 1920s marks the place and time where the Kless family first staked their claim in the Garden State diner business, a run that lasted more than four decades. The family purchased and installed a barrel-roof O'Mahony car in Springfield, which was replaced by a larger, more modern O'Mahony diner, on the same site, in 1932.

Albert Kless, who came from the Wurttemberg Baden (Stuttgart) area of Germany, arrived in the United States on April 15, 1889. A few years later, Albert brought his wife, Marie Shoemacher Kless, and his sister, Mathilda Kless, to America. A cabinet maker, Albert worked and lived with his family in Newark.

Albert and Marie had three sons: Albert Jr., Bill and Andrew. Bill, as a teenager, delivered groceries with a horse-drawn wagon. He married Lulu Apgar, whose family emigrated from Germany in the 1700s. Bill and Lulu opened two bakeries in Millburn and Flemington. They were successful and went on to buy and operate the aforementioned Kless Diner in Springfield.

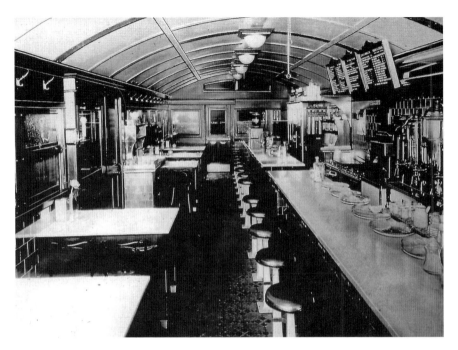

Interior of Kless Diner, Springfield. *Courtesy Bill Kless.*

By the mid-1940s, brother Andrew wanted to get into the diner business and worked for his brother Bill at the Springfield diner until the late 1940s. Around 1950, Andrew opened the Kless Diner at 1212 Springfield Avenue in Irvington. It was during this time frame that Bill and Lulu decided to change direction. They sold their diner in Springfield and retired to a twenty-acre farm in Chester, New Jersey. They spent several years on the farm but seized an opportunity to get into the lounge/restaurant business and bought the Dutch Kitchen in Ledgewood. After four years, they decided to get back into the diner business, sold the Dutch Kitchen and bought a lot in Irvington at Clinton Avenue and Washington Street. This became the site of the family's second diner in Irvington, built by Fodero, which opened April 18, 1955, at the corner of Clinton Avenue and Washington Street, adjacent to the town's bus station. The family also leased the Union Center Diner, located on Morris Avenue in Union, in 1959. The family's interest in that diner, which previously was known as the DeLuxe Diner, lasted until 1961.

By the mid-1960s, Andrew had sold the diner at 1212 Springfield Avenue. The new owners moved it to Chester, where it became known as the Chester Diner. After several years, the Kless diner was removed and replaced with a

Andrew (*right*) and Bill Kless, Kless Diner, Springfield, circa 1940. *Courtesy Bill Kless.*

new colonial-style diner. It later was expanded and remodeled and operates today on Route 206 in Chester.

The family sold the Clinton Avenue/Washington Street diner in late 1970, and it was moved—in four sections—to Beachwood, a borough in Ocean County, near Toms River. The December 13, 1970 edition of the *Asbury Park Press* reported that Walter Schmidt purchased the Kless diner to replace his Beachwood Diner, which was destroyed by a fire in the fall of that year. The new Beachwood, located near the intersection of Route 166 and Route 9, opened in January 1971. In 1988, the business changed its name to the Sand Castle Diner and continues to operate today in the same location.

Bill's son, also named Bill (Albert's grandson), worked for his dad briefly during his teenage years and today serves as the keeper of the family's archives. Grandson Bill never aspired to stay in the diner business, but he was a fascinated observer, especially during the early morning hours, when the local taverns closed and people were drawn to the diner.

Bill Kless, the father, was born on Broome Street in Newark on August 1, 1898. He died in 1961 and for a brief period Lulu ran the diner, until Andrew Kless bought out her share of the business in 1963.

## UNDER AN AWNING WITH THE SULTAN OF SWAT

Russell Van Atta (far left), born in Augusta, pitched for three seasons with the New York Yankees. Van Atta, a lefty, made his Major League debut on April 25, 1933, at Griffith Stadium in Washington, D.C., pitching a shutout and collecting four hits, as the Yankees beat the Senators, 16–0. During that 1933 season, Van Atta became a close friend of Babe Ruth (second from right), and they enjoyed many days hunting and fishing together in Sussex County. Following his baseball career, Van Atta turned to politics and was elected Sussex County sheriff on November 4, 1941. Ruth supported his friend's bid for sheriff, and one campaign appearance was captured in a photo under the awning of the old Newton Diner. Adrien Salvas, a photographer from Andover, took the picture in 1940. Floyd McCracken (third from right) owned the diner, located on Spring Street in downtown Newton. The eatery is significant as it's the first diner, built in 1937, by Master Diners. In recent years, it was known as Brenda's Diner, which closed in 2017. On June 8, 2018, it reopened as the Spring Diner. After serving as sheriff for one term, Van Atta was elected as a county freeholder and later became an executive with the V&H Oil Company of Newton. He died on October 10, 1986. George Herman Babe Ruth died on August 16, 1948.

Newton Diner. *Photograph from the collection of the Sussex County Historical Society, Newton.*

Andrew sold the diner after three years and died in 1967, and Lulu passed away in 1973.

Today, Bill Kless, the son and archive keeper, lives happily in Florida and occasionally enjoys going down the family's "memory lane" in the diner business. "My life has been good. I thank my parents for giving me a solid footing; not too many bumps in the road."

# "I Saw Him in My Dad"

Frank Frederick, in the early years of the twentieth century, worked for the Delaware, Lackawanna & Western Railroad. In 1924, Frederick's leg was broken in a train accident and healed badly. Frank's granddaughter Barbara (Frederick) Vazquez, recounting oral family history, said that Frank initially used the settlement money from his injury to go to barber school and opened a barbershop on Wright Street in Newark along with a partner named George Buce. The venture turned out to be brief. The two men decided to sell the barbershop and went their separate ways. Frederick then connected with another partner, Frank Soldo, and on November 24, 1926, they opened Frank's Diner at 264 Washington Avenue in Belleville.

The diner was located across the street from Peoples National Bank & Trust Company (today Valley National Bank), on the east side of Washington Avenue, the town's main business thoroughfare. The bank's president, a certain Mr. Aitken, was a regular lunchtime customer. The business became popular and profitable, which inspired the partners to open a second diner in Belleville at the intersection of Union and Belleville Avenues. This second diner partnership dissolved, with an agreement that Frank Frederick would keep and operate his namesake Washington Avenue establishment. The Belleville diner was open twenty-four hours a day. Frank worked the day shift, and his brother, Matt Frederick, held down the overnight hours. A brother-in-law, Frank Kress, worked part time as needed.

Tragedy struck during the early morning hours of May 6, 1940, when forty-year-old Frank Frederick was shot and killed during an armed robbery at Ziegler's Tavern, a "men's only" saloon, located in Belleville on Holmes Street, between Ralph and Main Streets. The *Newark Evening News*, in its May 6 and May 7, 1940 editions, covered the incident—the book *Belleville* (Images of America) by Nicole T. Canfora provides a photo and brief description of the tavern. Two thugs committed the crime, and they were later caught, convicted

Frank Frederick (*right*), Frank's Diner, Belleville. *Courtesy Barbara Frederick Vazquez.*

and sent to jail. In the aftermath of Frank's death, Barbara said the family tried leasing the diner operations, but without the presence of her grandfather, the business went downhill and soon closed.

Frank Frederick was the father of eight children, a member of the Holy Name Society of St. Peter's Church and the Knights of Columbus Belleville Council No. 835. He and his wife, Catherine Kress, both grew up in Pittston, Pennsylvania, a town on the Susquehanna River, but they met in New Jersey around 1919. "My grandfather was born in the United States, but his grandparents came from Prussia," Barbara said. "I don't know about my grandfather's cooking skills, but I guess that when you come from a large family, you learn how to cook. My grandmother would make a big platter of codfish cakes every Friday. My father [Robert Frederick, the oldest of the eight siblings] often helped at the diner after school." Barbara said her dad was forced to drop out of high school (in his senior year) to support the family, even though he had been considering college scholarship offers.

For fourteen years, Frank Frederick and his family operated a diner that welcomed bank presidents and working people. For many in Belleville, a slice of pie and a cup of coffee at Frank's Diner was a simple pleasure of daily life. And then, one day, unexpectedly, it all came to an end. It's a tragic story, but it's also a story of survival and a family's strength in the face of adversity.

"I always felt sad about how things turned out for my grandmother and my father," Barbara confessed. "Their lives were changed forever. My dad never spoke much about it. My grandmother told me there were some days when she didn't have enough food for the children. But I'm also very proud of them for keeping the family together. My grandmother was strong and independent. She knew she had to be tough to raise her family well, and she did a good job. Despite my grandfather's death, all eight children became good, solid, hardworking people with their own families. They all had a wonderful sense of humor, and we enjoyed many barbecues and good times together. I don't remember any of my aunts or uncles dwelling on their hard upbringing."

As for the grandfather she never knew, Barbara said that while growing up, she enjoyed hearing stories about how Frank Frederick was a "people person;" always happy and joking with his customers. "I can only say I would have loved to have known my grandfather, but I imagine I 'saw' him in my dad, aunts and uncles."

## "The Next Morning He Started All Over Again"

Throughout her life, Emily Diamond has been immersed in the diner business, first through her father and the Lexington Diner in Clifton and later through her husband and the Haledon Diner. She's been a witness to events that involve hardworking people with family roots in Germany, Poland and Greece and the rise of successful neighborhood diners in Passaic County.

Emily's dad, Henry Hansen, was born in 1902 in Flensburg, Germany, just south of Denmark. The Hansen family owned a restaurant named Osteebad, on the shores of the Baltic Sea, where Henry worked as a teenager. Being a restless young man, he found work on a cargo freighter that went to and from the United States. In 1922, he jumped ship when his vessel was docked in Galveston, Texas, and connected with a friend. Henry worked a series of jobs in the United States and Canada and then returned to Germany with money in his pockets. The Flensburg relatives and neighbors were impressed.

Germany, during the post–World War I years, suffered from hyperinflation and widespread unemployment. Sizing up the daunting economic conditions, Henry decided that North America was more to his liking. He once again crossed the Atlantic Ocean and landed in Canada, where he found work as a lumberjack. While in Canada, he received an unexpected call from a friend in Clifton. His buddy owned a luncheonette on Lexington Avenue and invited Henry to come to New Jersey and be his partner. Henry accepted the offer and headed south to the Garden State.

The two men worked together for several years, but then Henry spotted a new business opportunity and decided to go off on his own. He bought a small diner located on the corner of East Russell Street and Lexington Avenue in the Botany Village section of Clifton. He utilized the practical kitchen skills he had gained working at Osteebad, and the Lexington Diner soon became a big hit in the neighborhood. In 1932, Henry married Ruth Popeck, the daughter of Polish immigrants who had settled in the next-door town of Passaic. In the early 1930s, Henry moved the diner car one block south on Lexington Avenue to a piece of property with more space for a parking lot. The business gained momentum; he added a new dining room, and Henry was soon living the American dream as a successful entrepreneur.

Emily often worked the cash register and served as a waitress. She retains vivid memories of her dad and the business. Henry was a most gregarious man, and she can still picture him wearing his white kitchen apron and interacting with customers. "They were almost like family to him." Henry baked a large assortment of pies and made fresh fruit salad and rice pudding. Customer favorites at lunchtime were hot roasted loin of pork and roast beef sandwiches, sliced thin on a hard roll with brown gravy and a delicious pickle on the side. His customers also loved calf's liver. In later years, Henry expanded the menu to include lobster, clam chowder and fish platters. He would travel to the docks of Point Pleasant on Sunday nights and return early Monday mornings with fresh-caught seafood from his fishermen friends.

One day in the early 1950s, Emily caught the eye of a young man who was traveling through the Botany neighborhood. He had stopped at the gas station that was adjacent to the Lexington Diner. His name was Peter J. Diamondakos. His parents had lived on the Peloponnese peninsula of southern Greece and came to the United States around 1918. The Diamondakos family settled in Passaic and Americanized their last name to "Diamond." Peter struck up a conversation with Emily, which led to a first date, which led to them being married in 1955.

Peter, born in the United States, served in the U.S. Army Air Corps in the Pacific Theater during World War II. His parents owned a luncheonette on Market Street in Passaic, where he worked part time. By 1949, Peter had ambitions of starting his own business when he learned of

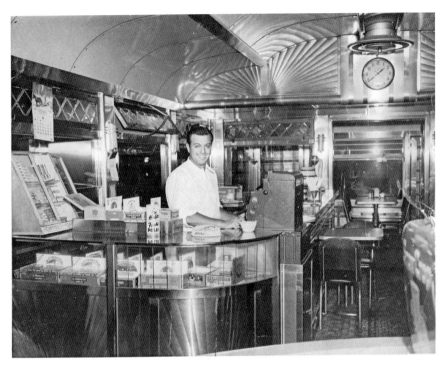

Peter Diamond, Haledon Diner. *Courtesy Emily Diamond.*

a diner for sale in Haledon, a suburb of Paterson. Peter, along with three relatives, formed a partnership and purchased the eatery. The Haledon Diner built up a loyal customer base from workers at nearby industries and warehouses and students from Paterson College (today's William Paterson University). After ten years, the business had grown to a point that a larger diner was needed. The partners acquired additional property at the corner of Haledon and Belmont Avenues and purchased a modern diner from their next-door neighbor, Paramount. The new diner included an attached cocktail lounge.

After forty-five years in the business, Henry Hansen, in 1969, sold the Lexington Diner. Today, the eatery continues to operate at the same spot on Lexington Avenue. Henry died in 1986. Peter Diamond and his partners sold their business in Haledon in the late 1970s. Today, a Dunkin' Donuts and an auto care shop occupy the site where the diner once stood. Peter died in 2012.

"A diner is an oasis where good food and friendships abound," Emily said. "My dad enjoyed the challenge of satisfying his customers and seeing happy

Haledon Diner. *Courtesy Emily Diamond.*

faces." Emily shared a final memory of Henry: "Even though he knew the food was very good, he rarely ate at his diner. Instead, he came home after 9:00 p.m. and preferred to sit at the kitchen table and eat whatever my mom had made for supper earlier that day. He loved this and it made him happy, because he could relax, talk with the family, and get away from the business for a while. And then the next morning he started all over again."

## Sarah's Six-Year Adventure

It was supposed to be a part-time waitress job to carry her through the summer of 2012, but it ended up spanning six years. It turned into an opportunity to interact with people she never would have known otherwise. The job drained her physically and emotionally, entertained her and frustrated her. And when asked to look back and reflect on this chapter of her life, Sarah Slominski smiled and said, "It was an adventure."

## The Second Hand Unwinds

The fate of Tom's Diner, located in Ledgewood at the intersection of Routes 46 and 10, remains uncertain, but it still was standing in July 2019. The Silk City car, built in Paterson around 1938, has fallen into serious disrepair. Tom Seretis, who manages the property for his family, said his grandfather purchased the diner, originally known as the Silver Dollar, in 1958. Cyndi Lauper included the diner in a scene from her 1984 music video *Time After Time*. Tom's dad, Frank, ran the business for many years. The diner closed not long after Frank died in 2004. Seretis said that he's optimistic and remains dedicated to reopening the diner but admitted that he faces numerous challenges. He also provided some family history, saying that his grandfather (also named Tom) came to the United States from Eleftheriani, Greece. His grandfather obtained a permit (dated March 28, 1936, at a cost of fifty dollars) from the Township of Denville to sell peanuts from a cart. "Twenty-two years later, he bought a Silk City dining car and named it Tom's Diner."

Tom's Diner. *Photo by M. Gabriele.*

Working as a waitress at the River Star Diner in her hometown of Hackettstown provided Sarah with a steady cash flow (lots of generous tips) during her days as a student at Warren County Community College and then at Cedar Crest College in Allentown, Pennsylvania. As its name suggests, the diner, which opened in the early 1990s, sits only a short distance from the banks of the Musconetcong River. "The diner is the center of the community. People are fussier about their food than anything under the sun," Sarah said. She added that she, too, is a selective eater. "My older sister is a pastry chef, so I'm very fussy about eating dessert. I've never liked eggs and I don't drink coffee." She said chicken parmigiana in various iterations—as a dinner platter, a Panini sandwich or a wrap—was her favorite item on the River Star Diner's menu.

The job was demanding, but she rose to the occasion. After a number of weeks, she learned the routines of the diner and the dining habits of her regular customers. "We saw the same people every day at the same time. They would usually order the same thing. It got to the point that we were concerned if they didn't show up for a few days." In turn, customers inquired about Sarah if she took a day off.

Her favorite cast of characters, three men who were buddies, dropped in at the diner on Sunday nights to engage in cheerful debates and trade good-natured insults while eating supper. Occasionally, they pestered the waitresses and drew them into the abrasive discussion. It became a weekly dose of entertainment. "This was dinner for them and a show for us," she said. While this rowdy trio brightened the mood inside the diner, Sarah said other customers also caught her attention. Her heart went out to the subdued, lonely people she came to know as regular patrons. They often ate alone at the diner during weeknights. When it came to boisterous customers, no one could top the energetic high school band students who descended on the diner after home football games.

In mid-2018, as she was working on the final stages of her master's degree, Sarah knew that her days at the diner were drawing to an end. It was time to move on. "I was done. I realized I couldn't do it anymore." July 8, 2018, was her last day as a waitress. The next day, she started her job in the Sussex County Library system.

Interviewed at her library desk in late September 2018, she acknowledged missing her diner customers and associates. Her six-year adventure of getting to know fussy customers and lonely customers and loud customers is an education she won't soon forget.

When asked what happened when she said goodbye to the River Star Diner on July 8, Sarah's face became flush; she looked down at her desk and hesitated before answering. "I cried. I cried a lot. Change is hard."

# "Not as Easy as It Looks"

The passage of family diner ownership—parents to a son or daughter, an aunt and uncle to a niece or nephew—is a reassuring aspect of New Jersey diner history. Passing the torch from one generation to the next offers the hope that the diner will remain in familiar hands, providing a measure of continuity for customers.

One example of this succession occurred in early 2018, when Panagioti ("Pete") Apostolou, the owner of the Blairstown Diner, passed away on January 28. He had run the diner for nearly thirty years. As expected, his son, Peter, took the reins. It was a smooth transition, but "it's not as easy as it looks," Peter said, with eyes open wide during an interview in September 2018. "This diner is a living, breathing thing. People rely on this place."

It was a Sunday morning when Peter sat down to chat, and the diner was buzzing with a full house of customers. Parties of three, four and five kept arriving. As they made their way through the entrance, the young woman at the cash register gave a quick look around the diner and said, "It will be about ten or fifteen minutes. Is that OK?" Members of each group nodded their heads in consent and waited to be seated. At the same time, customers stopped in for their take-out orders. The kitchen staff worked feverishly to keep pace with the breakfast crowd.

Peter's dad was born in Greece in March 1941. At age twenty-four, he came to the United States without much money but was determined to find employment and make a life for himself. He worked at various diners as a dish washer, a busboy and a short-order cook. He saved enough money to buy his own business in Spring Valley, New York: the Red Eagle Diner. He sold that eatery in 1989 and in 1990 acquired the Blairstown Diner, which was built by Paramount.

"The success of this diner is due to my dad," Peter continued. "He made it all work, and he did it his own way. He had his own methods for doing business." Peter worked with his father at the diner for fifteen years. As an outpost in Warren County, fifteen miles east of the Delaware Water Gap, the diner enjoys fame among movie fans, as it appears in the 1980

Blairstown Diner. *Photo by M. Gabriele.*

horror film *Friday the 13th*. As a result, it's become a destination for devotees of the movie.

Peter said that in 2015, he decided he needed a change and started his own business, a pool and spa maintenance and repair company. His father initially was a bit uneasy regarding this move, but then a funny thing happened. "We became best friends," Peter said. Perhaps it was Peter's decision to establish a separate business that provided the space to allow him and his dad to discuss serious family matters, like managing the diner business. The plan was clear cut from his dad's perspective. "I was always aware that one day I would take over the diner. That's what my dad expected and that's what he wanted me to do."

A framed photograph of Panagioti Apostolou is displayed in the kitchen—a symbolic reminder of his lasting legacy. Peter is a most capable, dutiful son, but he quickly learned that following in his father's footsteps would be challenging. There were numerous expectations to live up to, and he had his own ideas for running the business. Peter said staffing—finding durable, reliable people—is his biggest ongoing concern. Now it's his responsibility to react to everyday situations on the fly, such as working in the kitchen if one of his cooks calls in sick or addressing unforeseen maintenance issues. On top of all that, he's also managing his pool and spa company.

THE BLAIRSTOWN DINER OPENED on September 30, 1949. Charles Simonson, the first owner, ran a full-page ad in the Thursday, September 29, 1949 edition of the *Blairstown Press* to trumpet his grand opening. "You are cordially invited to visit our new diner and enjoy the home-like meals we serve," the ad copy read. "Whether you want a sandwich or a full-course meal, you will find us ready to serve you twenty-four hours a day."

The basic design of the diner today looks similar to when it debuted in 1949, with its glass brick rounded corners. Pictured in the full-page ad, the diner had two front doors and two large bay windows for take-out orders. A transportation invoice, dated August 24, 1949, documented that Charles Simonson paid Paramount $515 for the "transport of diner number 607 to Blairstown." Paramount, in a boxed item on the invoice, described its "custom-built dining cars" as having "all-steel frames with well-seasoned lumber, tile and marble, porcelain ceilings and fully equipped."

A one-column news article in the paper's September 29, 1949 edition described the diner as "the newest type stainless steel construction. It is located in the center of town on Route 8 [today's Route 94]….Simonson is well qualified to manage his new undertaking. He spent his whole life in the restaurant business, coming here from the Belvidere Diner, where he was employed for the past four years." Born in Newark in 1921, Charles Simonson served in the merchant marines in Hawaii during World War II. After the war, he returned to New Jersey and began working at the Belvidere Diner.

The Blairstown diner drew customers from throughout Warren County, as well as from across the Delaware River in the Keystone State. Local customers during those early years also came from John Hill's Amusement Hall, which was located across the street from the diner. The hall, which had a bar, featured Saturday night square dancing with a live band. Patrons dropped into the diner for a late snack after working up an appetite from square dancing.

In August 1955, the remnants of Hurricane Diane flooded Blairstown. The Blairstown Diner was forced to close on August 19, 1955, when floodwaters rose along Route 94. The historic covered bridge that spanned the Delaware River between Columbia, New Jersey, and Portland, Pennsylvania (it opened on January 16, 1869), was demolished during the storm.

A September 1958 edition of the *Blairstown Press* published a story that celebrated the diner's ongoing success as a local gathering spot. "Charles Simonson opened the diner in September 1949 and it became popular so quickly that he enlarged the dining room so that it will now seat fifty.

All the food is home cooked and includes a variety to please the most discriminating taste. Homemade doughnuts are made each night and are a very popular item."

The Simonson family sold the diner to Gail and Carl Dieffenbach in 1983. They owned it for several years and then sold it to the Lang family. As mentioned earlier, Apostolou purchased the diner in 1990. Simonson died on April 24, 1988, and Gail Dieffenbach died on October 24, 2018.

The diner underwent a major renovation project in 2005. PMC Diners, the descendant of Paramount, upgraded the roof, completely redesigned the façade, removed the diner sign on the roof and eliminated the two doors and bay windows, creating a single front vestibule entrance in the center of the structure.

Sitting at the diner during the Sunday morning interview, Peter Apostolou maintained a positive outlook regarding his stewardship of the Blairstown Diner and seemed to be taking things in stride, despite his hectic schedule. "I can't tell you what tomorrow will bring," he said with a disarming, philosophical smile. "Who knows what will happen from here. I have a wife, two kids, one dog and two businesses. It's easy to be stressed out, but that changes nothing." Much like his dad was determined to put his mark on the

Blairstown Diner, circa 2000. *Courtesy Larry Cultrera.*

diner's business, Peter, in his own way, is equally determined to sustain it and take the diner to new levels.

The strong current of the Paulinskill River flows under the historic Blairstown Footbridge, located behind the diner. Black bears, deer and raccoons ramble throughout the woods that line Route 521. Fans of the movie *Friday the 13th* occasionally pass through town and stop to take pictures. Trucks, vans and cars travel on Route 94. Tomorrow morning, a living, breathing thing known as the Blairstown Diner will awaken, just as it has for the last seventy years. People rely on this place. Breakfast will be served starting at 6:00 a.m. Customers might need to wait for ten or fifteen minutes before they can be seated, but that will be fine. All is well in Blairstown. All is well.

# An Intersection of Two Roads and Many Lives

Tom and Sandi Zikas built a forty-one-year career at a crossroads—the intersection of Routes 46 and 519 in Belvidere—as the owners of the Crossroads Diner. As they had planned, this chapter of their lives came to an end at 2:00 p.m. on Sunday, July 1, 2018. It was time to retire from the diner business. Longtime customers packed the diner that day, bidding farewell to Sandi and Tom.

Rock-and-roll tunes served as the sentimental background music that day. Waitresses wore black-and-pink poodle skirts. For Sandi, a parade of former waitresses that stopped in to say so long became the highlight of the final day. She recalled that most of them met first (and second) husbands while working at the diner.

Sandi said that for nearly a year, prior to the diner's final day, she and Tom entertained a number of offers from local entrepreneurs that expressed an interest in buying and operating the diner. "It didn't happen. All these discussions fell through," she said. As a result, the Zikas family sold the property to the Dunkin' Donuts chain.

The Crossroads opened in 1956, built by the Campora Dining Car Company of Kearny—believed to be the only diner produced by this short-lived manufacturer. During the 1950s, prior to the construction of interstate highways, the Crossroads served as a Greyhound Bus stop. In the early 1980s, the diner was the happening place at 2:00 a.m. on Friday and Saturday nights, when local dance clubs closed. The diner became "the real party spot" after a wild night of dancing, drinking, romance and

*Left*: Tom and Sandi Zikas, final day at the Crossroads Diner. *Photo by M. Gabriele.*

*Below*: Crossroads Diner. *Photo by M. Gabriele.*

carousing. "Everyone came here," Sandi said, recalling those whirlwind episodes. "Everyone felt good." In the years that followed, the fast-dancing night owls remained loyal customers and began showing up with their spouses and kids for breakfast, lunch and supper.

During more sedate daytime business hours, people in this corner of Warren County gathered at the Crossroads to catch up on local news and gossip, according to diner regular Karen Huff Kilts. A member of the class of 1969 at Warren Hills Regional High School and a 1971 graduate of Warren County Technical School, Kilts said she frequented the diner, usually for lunch, an average of three days a week. "The food was always good," she said during a September 2018 phone interview. "It was a comfortable place for people to meet. We would sit there and laugh and make new friends. Farmers came in and told us stories. Everyone had a favorite waitress. All those friendships and chit chat—that's what I'll miss the most."

Kilts began to weep when she recalled a special Crossroads diner friendship with a former instructor at Warren County Technical School and his wife. She occasionally joined them for lunch, and they would reminisce about her classmates and his experiences as a teacher. The man's wife died just before Christmas 2016. After a number of weeks, Kilts saw him at the diner in early 2017, this time sitting alone at his usual booth.

"I asked if I could join him, and he said 'sure.' We began to talk about his family. He said he enjoyed the conversation because it brought back happy memories of his wife. He always had a story to tell."

Their final encounter came just weeks before the Crossroads closed. Once again, she spotted him at lunchtime in the same booth, but this time he was in tears. "Unfortunately, I've lost touch with him," Kilts lamented. "I don't know if I'll ever see him again."

As of July 2019, the vacant Crossroads was still standing at its spot on Route 46.

# A Long Night's Journey to Say Goodbye

On May 31, 2017, there was a heavy-hearted gathering to mark the final day of business for another diner: the Egg Platter. Master Diners manufactured the Egg Platter, which opened in the mid-1940s and originally was known as Geier's City Line Diner—a reference to its location on Crooks Avenue, the boundary line between Paterson and Clifton.

## HUNTERS AND FISHERMEN

Ever since they opened Yetter's Diner on April 18, 1986, located at the intersection of Route 206 and Route 15 in Augusta, Sussex County, Spiros and Roula Hatzinas mark the seasons for their busiest times of the year: autumn for hunting and spring for fishing. "We open at 4:30 a.m. and we still have lines out the door," Spiros said. Knight's Diner, a barrel-roof lunch wagon, operated here from 1915 to 1945. In 1945, a Dutchman named Lawrence Yetter bought the site and installed a new diner. The Hatzinas family purchased the business and removed Yetter's Diner but kept the name. They installed the current Mediterranean-style diner, previously known as the Derby Diner, which they transported in three sections to Augusta from where it had stood on Route 17 in Rutherford. The Hatzinas family arrived in the United States from Greece in 1978. Spiros and Roula said they are making plans for retirement. When they step down, their son, Tommy (Athanasios), will run the business.

Yetter's Diner. *Photo by M. Gabriele.*

The Egg Platter, owned by the Dermatis family, was a "first cousin" to the popular Bendix Diner, located in Hasbrouck Heights at the intersection of Routes 17 and 46. (Master also built the Bendix.) The diner added an extension for an additional dining area in September 1984. In the year leading up to its closing, local news stories reported that the site would be developed as a four-story, multiuse building, which meant that the diner would be removed.

John Baeder, *Market Tower, Jersey City N.J., 2007*, oil on canvas. *Courtesy Bernarducci Gallery, New York.*

Legends Diner, Secaucus. *Photo by M. Gabriele.*

Angelo's Glassboro Diner. *Photo by M. Gabriele.*

Johnny Prince's Famous Bayway Diner, Linden. *Photo by M. Gabriele.*

Andover Diner. *Photo by M. Gabriele.*

Paul's Diner, Mountain Lakes. *Photo by M. Gabriele.*

Whitman Diner, Blackwood. *Photo by M. Gabriele.*

Meadows Diner, Blackwood. *Photo by M. Gabriele.*

George Campbell, Broad Street Diner, Keyport. *Photo by M. Gabriele.*

Cherry Hill Diner. *Photo by M. Gabriele.*

New Berlin Diner. *Photo by M. Gabriele.*

54 Diner, Route 54, Buena. *Photo by M. Gabriele.*

Princess Maria Diner, Wall Township. *Photo by M. Gabriele.*

New Monmouth Diner, Middletown. *Photo by M. Gabriele.*

Time to Eat Diner, Bridgewater. *Photo by M. Gabriele.*

Jimmy Greberis (*left*) and Eric Evers at the Summit Diner. *Photo by M. Gabriele.*

Jackson Hole Diner, Englewood. *Photo by M. Gabriele.*

Anthony Musarra (*left*) and Vinnie Altier, Canton, Michigan. *Courtesy Anthony Musarra.*

Randolph Diner. *Photo by M. Gabriele.*

Vincentown Diner. *Photo by M. Gabriele.*

Marlton Diner. *Photo by M. Gabriele.*

Menlo Park Diner, Edison. *Photo by M. Gabriele.*

Spinning Wheel Diner, Lebanon. *Photo by M. Gabriele.*

Phily Diner, Runnemede. *Photo by M. Gabriele.*

City Diner, Jersey City. *Photo by M. Gabriele.*

Montclair Diner. *Photo by M. Gabriele.*

Club Diner,
Bellmawr. *Photo
by M. Gabriele.*

Oakland Diner.
*Photo by M.
Gabriele.*

Victoria Diner,
Branchville. *Photo
by M. Gabriele.*

White Star Diner, Plainfield. *Photo by M. Gabriele.*

Mainline Pizzeria, Little Falls (built by Manno). *Photo by M. Gabriele.*

West Side Diner, Denville. *Photo by M. Gabriele.*

Short-order cooks at the Truck Stop Diner, Kearny. *Photo by M. Gabriele.*

Steven Kolovos and Tom Philis remained stoic on that last day, resigned to the diner's fate. They had been the grill men at the Egg Platter since 1977 and, just like they had done for four decades, they faithfully turned out eggs, pancakes, French toast, corned beef hash, potatoes and bacon for the last time on this Wednesday morning of May 31.

This author stopped in that day at 7:00 a.m. and ordered coffee and two eggs over easy with bacon, just for old time's sake. The grill sizzled, waitresses laughed, coffee flowed and saucers and dishes chattered—all the familiar diner sights and sounds that soon would be silenced.

Gerhard Hiemer was a diner regular who became the president of his family's business, Hiemer and Company stained glass studio, located on the Clifton side of Crooks Avenue, just two blocks away from the Egg Platter. Hiemer recalled that prior to the arrival of Master's Geier's City Line Diner, there was a lunch wagon that operated on the same site, with an exterior "skirt" that covered the wagon's wheels.

As reported online by NorthJersey.com, there was one particularly dedicated (and hungry) patron who knew that he simply couldn't miss the Egg Platter's last day. Bob Ogorzaly, a former Paterson resident living in Charlottesville, Virginia, began his pilgrimage to the diner just after midnight. The fifty-one-year-old Ogorzaly said that as a lad growing up in Paterson, he and his parents were regulars at the Egg Platter. As mentioned in the introduction chapter, he drove seven hours to arrive at the diner minutes after it opened.

Sitting at the counter, feeling sentimental and famished from his long trek, Ogorzaly was determined to have his fill—a feast that included plates of eggs, home fries, French toast and coffee. He returned to the diner later that day to collect a few Taylor Ham and egg sandwiches "for the road," according to the NorthJersey.com story. Well done, Mr. Ogorzaly. You seized the moment, went more than the extra mile, got your money's worth and bid farewell to the diner of your childhood. You kept the faith.

The Egg Platter was torn down on November 15–16, 2018.

# A Plethora of Frothy Shakes on Campus

Sacred Heart University, Fairfield, Connecticut, held a ribbon-cutting ceremony on October 16, 2017, to formally celebrate the opening of JP's Diner, which was built in six sections by DeRaffele. It was a gala affair with music, balloons and speeches by various dignitaries. Students joyfully welcomed the crimson diner to the campus.

Wait a minute—a diner located on a college campus in Connecticut, manufactured by a company in New York? This isn't a New Jersey story.

*Au contraire*! There is an important Garden State connection for this tale, beginning with the diner's name. The initials "JP" stand for John J. Petillo, PhD, the president of Sacred Heart and a Jersey guy through and through. Petillo grew up in North Newark; attended St. Francis Xavier Parish, located at the intersection of Bloomfield and Roseville Avenues; and is a graduate of Essex Catholic High School, class of 1964. His New Jersey business résumé includes executive positions at the University of Medicine and Dentistry of New Jersey, the Newark Alliance, First Union Insurance Services, the Tribus Companies and Blue Cross Blue Shield. He also served as the chancellor and chief executive officer of Seton Hall University and Immaculate Conception Seminary, both in South Orange, and was a chancellor for administration at the Archdiocese of Newark.

During his formative years, Petillo, along with his family and friends, regularly ate at diners and ice cream parlors in the Newark area. "Diners were always an attraction for my parents, because they knew they would

JP's Diner, Sacred Heart University, Fairfield, Connecticut. *Photo by M. Gabriele.*

get a reliable meal at a good price," he said during an on-campus interview inside the diner. As a youngster, his favorite meal was a hamburger, French fries and a milkshake.

Petillo arrived at Sacred Heart in March 2009 and became the dean of the university's Jack Welch College of Business, named in honor of the former chairman and chief executive officer of General Electric. The university tapped Petillo as interim president in October 2010, and he was named president in March 2011. He took the helm at Sacred Heart and guided the university through the initial phases of a major expansion of its facilities and academic programs. The expansion plan identified the need for another dining facility to accommodate the growing student body. Late one night during this period, an idea came to Petillo. "I thought we needed something very different, something that the students would really enjoy." His Jersey instincts kicked in, and he decided to build an authentic diner on the Sacred Heart campus.

He admitted that, at first, his idea of a diner on campus drew a few puzzled looks from faculty and board members. Petillo pointed to a precedent for having a diner on a college campus. Montclair State University, on October 23, 2001, unveiled its Red Hawk Diner, which was built by Kullman. Montclair State, at the time, hailed it as the first and only diner to operate on a college campus. (Since then, Henry's Diner, a storefront eatery on the campus of Rutgers University, opened on September 9, 2013.) Petillo won over his colleagues, and the university formed a committee to explore the diner concept and then considered various designs for the eatery. The committee selected DeRaffele to design and manufacture the structure.

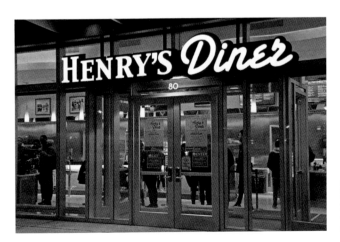

Henry's Diner, Rutgers University, New Brunswick. *Photo by M. Gabriele.*

Following the October 2017 ribbon-cutting event, the diner, with seating for 110 people and additional outdoor patio seating for 40, quickly caught on with the student body as well as with people in the surrounding Fairfield community. Soon there were lines out the door. As a spot on the campus social scene, students enjoy spending time at the diner during late-night hours. Another relocated Jersey guy, former Lake Hopatcong resident Mark M. Tammone, resident district manager for Chartwells Dining Services, which oversees the diner's daily operation, said that milkshakes became the rage among the students. Tammone estimated that the diner sold more than five thousand shakes between November 14 and Christmas Day. He said the diner's menu contains classics such as egg dishes, hamburgers, sandwiches, wraps and desserts.

# CENTRAL NEW JERSEY

## "Jack Made It More than a Diner"

Nick and Maria Kallas's success story at the Broad Street Diner in Keyport began precisely at 6:00 a.m. on January 30, 2015, when a customer placed an order for eggs Benedict. Eleven months later, *Star-Ledger* columnist Peter Genovese arrived at the front entrance to proclaim that Broad Street had earned the prestigious title as New Jersey's Best Diner for 2015. When weighed against forty semifinalists and ten finalists, as Genovese wrote in an online article posted on December 17, 2015, no diner "combined great food, friendly service and convivial atmosphere in one package like the Broad Street Diner."

Since that proclamation, Nick and Maria have seen their business skyrocket. When they took time out to catch their breath and do an interview in the diner's kitchen, they were all smiles and still appreciative of the award.

The story behind Maria and Nick's achievements at Broad Street Diner can be traced back to numerous family connections. Maria's dad, Billy Niotis, worked as a chef on ships in Greece's navy during the 1960s. Billy Niotis came to America and in 1970 partnered with Nick's dad, John Kallas, to operate the Parsonage Diner in Menlo Park. The diner closed in 1996 when its lease ran out, and it was removed from its location at the intersection of Route 27 and Parsonage Road in Menlo Park to make way for a chain drugstore.

Maria and Nick Kallas, Broad Street Diner. *Photo by M. Gabriele.*

Nick started as a busboy at the diner at age fourteen. He later expressed an interest in food preparation and learned the craft of being a short-order cook. John Kallas ran the front of the Parsonage Diner, while Billy Niotis was in charge of the kitchen. Aside from the Parsonage Diner, the family's diner legacy includes Maria's grandfather, Gus Milonas Niotis, who years ago operated diners in Cranford, and her brother, Michael Niotis, who runs the Seaport Diner in Elizabeth.

During the early Parsonage Diner days, Maria and Nick knew each other through the family friendship and business partnership. Nick said Maria's dad taught him the basics of cooking, and he used those skills for a six-month stint at his family's hotel restaurant in Greece. When he returned to New Jersey, he reconnected with Maria, the relationship blossomed into a romance and they married on February 15, 1998. After the Parsonage Diner closed, Nick went into business with relatives and partners at the Windsor Diner in Clark, where he ran the kitchen. The Windsor Diner ceased operations in 2012 and was remodeled as a restaurant.

Confident in their skills and experience, Nick and Maria were ready to start their own business. They heard about an eatery for sale in Keyport, known at the time as Stanley's Seaport Diner, built by O'Mahony. They fell in love with the place and purchased it in November 2014. Two months later, after a series of renovations, the diner opened for business.

These days, the diner is home to a strange character holding a pink guitar, wearing a bright-yellow jacket and bearing a strong resemblance to the king of rock-and-roll, who never seems to leave the building. Elvis aside, when it comes to noteworthy individuals, a special visitor arrived at the Broad Street Diner on November 9, 2017. George Campbell had just celebrated his 100th birthday. His daughter, Tricia McAvoy, made arrangements for him to visit the Broad Street Diner. George was employed at Jerry O'Mahony's factory in Elizabeth, beginning in 1947 until the business closed in May 1956, so given the vintage of when the Broad Street was built (around 1952), it's possible that George did work on the Broad Street Diner in the O'Mahony factory.

Challa bread French toast, Broad Street Diner, Keyport. *Photo by M. Gabriele.*

Broad Street Diner, Keyport. *Photo by M. Gabriele.*

Campbell, born in Perth Amboy on October 10, 1917, joined the navy in December 1941, right after the attack on Pearl Harbor. He was stationed in Guam during World War II, serving as a sheet metal worker to repair planes for the Pacific fleet. When the war ended, Campbell returned to New Jersey; married Kathleen Coogan, who hailed from Ireland; and landed a job at the O'Mahony plant as a "tin knocker," a term used by Campbell to describe his work in sheet metal. When the Elizabeth factor closed, Campbell and a number of associates led by Joseph A. Montano, the O'Mahony plant manager, established a short-lived company in 1956 called Mahony Diners Inc., which was located on Jacobus Avenue in Kearny. Gutman, in his book, wrote that this new business constructed only four diners and closed in 1957. Campbell remained active as a steel worker and became part of the construction crew that built the Twin Towers of the World Trade Center in New York City.

THE HISTORY OF THE Broad Street Diner dates back to the 1920s. There have been three diners located at the same Broad Street location. *Keyport in the Twentieth Century*, a book by Timothy E. Regan, provides photos of the first two lunch wagon eateries. The Palace Lunch is pictured in a photo dated July 4, 1928, showing Keyport's "Decoration Day" (Memorial Day) parade. (This same image is depicted on the interior wall of the Broad Street Diner.) A second photo in the book shows a different diner, Stanley's Ideal Diner, at the same spot. Anne Conway, a lifelong Keyport resident born in 1923, said her father and mother, Stanley and Helen Zabriski, purchased this second diner in 1936 from a man named Walter Walsh. The lunch wagon originally was known as the Ideal Diner, and Stanley added his name after buying the place. As a teenager, Anne worked with her parents. In those days, the diner opened at 6:00 a.m. and closed at 7:00 p.m. "Hard work, long hours and lots of laughs," she recalled.

The diner thrived as a popular spot in downtown Keyport, and that success inspired Stanley and Helen to order a new diner from O'Mahony. Stanley's "modern, air conditioned" diner held its grand opening on February 16, 1953. A business and industry section of the August 25, 1954 edition of the *Bayshore News* offered words of praise for the eatery. "Stanley's Diner is representative of the modern American diner at its best, and its steady growth and unwavering popularity are no accident," an article in this edition stated. "They are the result of careful planning, personal interest and untiring devotion to the serving of good food, skillfully prepared and served in attractive, friendly surroundings. Stanley's Diner, under the capable management of Mr. and Mrs. Stanley Zabriski, has been catering to the public's food desires and preferences for a long time. It remained for America to popularize and perfect the diner, a type of restaurant as American as apple pie and ice cream, and for the individualistic touch to be developed by the personal abilities and attributes of the management under which it operates."

Stanley Zabriski died in 1958. Anne, along with her husband, John ("Jack") Conway, who learned the diner trade from her father, assumed ownership of the diner. Anne said that Jack enjoyed the business, especially the interaction with customers. Jack had worked at Bell Telephone for fourteen years and welcomed the change of scenery. After operating the place for nearly three decades, Jack and Anne decided to sell the diner, with March 29, 1986, marking their final day of business. Helen Zabriski died three years later. There were several intermediate owners who operated the eatery until Nick and Maria came along in 2014.

When they said goodbye to the diner, Anne and Jack Conway expressed their appreciation for the Keyport community's many years of support. "We've seen three generation of families come in here, and it's the people

Stanley's Diner. *Courtesy Anne Conway.*

that have made this worth it." Anne said, quoted in a story in the April 2, 1986 edition of *The Independent*. "If there is any one thing that I will remember, it's the customers," Jack stated in the same story. "We always had the greatest customers in the world."

Anne said that Jack's health was the main factor in the decision to part with the diner. He suffered a serious heart attack in 1983 while working at the eatery and spent many months convalescing. Anne admitted that it was a difficult decision to sell the business because of the sentimental attachments she and Jack had with the diner. She still enjoys an occasional meal at the Broad Street Diner. "They're doing a good job," Anne said of Nick and Maria. "They're very nice people. I'm just happy that the diner is still around and still popular."

Jack Conway died of a second heart attack on Friday, September 13, 1991, while sitting in the pews of Holy Family Roman Catholic Church in Union Beach. A newspaper column, "Off the Record," by David Thaler, the editor and publisher of *The Independent*, provided a sentimental commentary on Jack's passing and the end of an era:

> *When Jack Conway died last month a little bit of Keyport died with him. If you wanted to know what was happening in Keyport, you went to Stanley's. Jack was the short-order cook. A burly man, he stood in front of the grill and held court with the regular customers who sat at the counter. His day started at five in the morning and it ended at eleven every night, six days a week. There was a special [dish] for every day of the week and it never changed from week to week. Jack knew the regulars, knew their life histories. His sometimes-gruff exterior belied a warmth that made his customers his friends. He gave Stanley's its personality. He made it more than a diner.*

# Diners by Design

Mark Blasch, a 1982 graduate of the University of Cincinnati, is an architect who has witnessed firsthand the transition of diner construction in New Jersey, from factory-built, modular, prefabricated cars to grand, site-built eateries. Kullman Industries hired Blasch in 1991, and his first assignment was to work on the third and current iteration of Tick Tock Diner, located on the westbound side of Route 3 in Clifton. Blasch confessed it was the first time he had ever drafted plans for a diner, but he was a quick study and dove into the intricacies of modular, prefabricated design.

"Designing a diner in a [factory-built] modular concept is very detailed work," he said. Sitting at the drawing board in his home, which is located in the town of Rocky Hill in Somerset County, he explained that a modular, prefabricated diner "is more like a piece of furniture than a building. It's designed to be picked up and moved. But there are limitations with the size of the rooms, kitchens and eating areas."

He landed at Kullman at the beginning of the end of the twentieth century's era of manufacturing diners in factories. The business was changing, and diner owners now demanded larger, more lavish structures with spacious dining areas. This called for diners to be designed as site-built structures. The *New York Times*, in its July 18, 1993 edition ("Diner Builder Takes a New Tack"), reported on Kullman's business strategy and transition into new markets. Robert Kullman, the third-generation president and chief executive officer of the company, pointed out that, by the early 1990s, while there was a drastic shift in annual diner demand and the company did migrate into new business sectors, "we never stopped building diners. Diners became one of our markets, not our only business."

Blasch demystified the practicalities of the design process, saying that one of the first items to consider is a route and logistics survey of the site for setting the diner modules. "When you're designing a diner, you have to meet the expectations of the customer [the diner owner] in terms of the style and size of the building, and the budget." He said a designer needs to take an "overview perspective" when it comes to the dimensions of the building, zoning ordinances, the layout of the property, parking requirements for customers, the location of the diner and even the flow of traffic, especially if the structure is situated near an intersection of highways.

During his days at Kullman, Blasch frequently visited the factory floor to discuss projects with colleagues like Umberto Benvinuto, the head of the metal shop; Carmino DeSilva, the foreman; Michael Kosinski, the welding foreman; and Frank "Che Che" Aloe, the transportation and rigging foreman. Blasch said these interactions proved to be beneficial for all involved and helped to improve the production process.

He spent fifteen years with Kullman and then went on to explore new ventures. As he networked with business associates, Blasch connected with Bill Kontas, the president of United Diner Construction Inc., based in Philadelphia. Working with United Diner, Blasch designed JB's Diner on 33 in Farmingdale, which opened in May 2017, located on the site previously

Mark Blasch. *Photo by M. Gabriele.*

occupied by the Apollo Diner at the intersection of Routes 33 and 34, and the Brooklawn Diner in Camden County. Other dazzling Garden State diners built by United Diner include the Jersey Diner in Cinnaminson, the Phily Diner in Runnemede, Pete's Diner in Williamstown, the Star Diner and Café in North Wildwood and the Silver Coin Diner in Hammonton.

Blasch is most proud of the knowledge he's accumulated on the proper handling of stainless steel—the signature element of a New Jersey diner. "You have to know how stainless steel works," he said, explaining that an extensive amount of time goes into creating "sunbursts" and other artistic features in the sheet metal. It involves understanding how light plays against the curves of concave and convex metal shapes. Today, Blasch is an independent architect and does an extensive amount of work with United Diner. He said that in his career, he's been involved in the design work on more than thirty diners throughout New Jersey, plus fifty renovation projects and expansions.

He outlined fundamental differences between site-built and factory-built diners. Today's site-built diners aren't bound by the size limitations of golden age, factory-built diners. Because they're literally constructed on a piece of property rather than inside a factory, site-built diners have the luxury of being expansive structures, with high ceilings, picture windows and large booths. By contrast, manufacturers were ever mindful of a factory-built diner's overall height, width, weight and length because the eateries were transported on roadways (in sections or as a single unit) by tractor trailer trucks. Golden age designers took advantage of the tighter dimensions to create cozy, intimate interior atmospheres.

Once they were trucked to a given location, factory-built diners typically sat atop a foundation with either a crawl space or basement, which provided the area for utility hookups, especially plumbing. Site-built diners often are constructed on a concrete slab-on-grade base, which is useful in locations with poor soil or groundwater concerns.

Many site-built diners have a perimeter parapet wall on their rooftops, a design feature that serves two purposes: to provide a colorful, eye-catching appeal to motorists and to cosmetically hide rooftop equipment. There is little installation of prefabricated materials or components for today's site-built diners. Today, prefabricated modules are used mostly in building construction projects that have numerous, highly repetitive spaces, like hotel restrooms. Kitchen design is unique to each diner and is highly dependent on the menu, Blasch said.

Terrazzo floors are seldom seen these days for site-built diners (too expensive and a dwindling number of terrazzo craftspeople). Non-magnetic stainless steel (such as Grade 304, which is alloyed with nickel and chromium) is specified for exterior and interior panels because it holds its polish and has more long-term resistance to corrosion and surface pitting. While long counters were once a crowning interior feature of factory-built diners, site-built diners tend to have limited counter space to create more room for booths and tables.

# Big Rigs and Hungry Truckers

It was the proverbial darkest hours before dawn on September 21, 2018, at the corner of South Wood Avenue and Morses Mill Road in Linden when Jess opened Johnny Prince's Famous Bayway Diner. As soon as she unlocked the door, turned on the lights and fired up the grill, a crowd of truck drivers swooped in to order breakfast. "They're always watching and waiting for me," she said with a grin. "It's nice to be popular."

The diner sits in the Union County town's industrial complex, home to the Phillips 66 Bayway refinery, the Linden Co-Generating plant, Linden

Airport and a handful of energy companies and distribution warehouses. With seven fixed stools and one movable chair, tight interior dimensions and no booths, the Bayway Diner is a modern reincarnation of a lunch wagon (sans wheels). The structure is actually a remodeled trailer, retrofitted with stainless steel exterior panels, a tile floor and cooking equipment.

Small talk and salutations fill the eatery, which is dominated by regular customers. Truckers take turns occupying spots at the counter, shuttling in and out, bumping into one another and politely excusing themselves and picking up coffee and sandwiches to go. By 6:00 a.m., the phone is ringing every few minutes, and Jess, the manager and head chef, relays take-out orders to her assistants, Elvis and Heather. "Good morning, Tom. The usual? OK, see you in a few." The phone conversation revealed that "the usual" for Tom was Pork Roll with eggs and cheese on a roll.

At quarter past six o'clock that morning, Nuhem and Manny, drivers for the nearby Wayfair warehouse, a distributor of home furnishings, and Noel, a terminal dispatcher for a shipping company in the industrial park, settled in at one end of the counter to enjoy breakfast. Manny ordered a platter of eggs over easy, bacon, a sausage patty, French toast and fried potatoes. It was colossal—an impressive heavy-duty power breakfast.

Nuhem, Manny and Noel (*left to right*), breakfast at Bayway Diner. *Photo by M. Gabriele.*

Noel, the dispatcher, offered his thoughts on why truck drivers enjoy diners in general and the Bayway in particular. "The convenience," he said. "Truckers like to get in and out fast. They want to get back on the road. The food's good and it's homemade. Good coffee. Diners are comfortable places if you have time to sit and talk for a few minutes. And Jess," emphasizing her name at the end of his remarks, leaving no doubt that she was the most important of all his points.

Jess started working at the Bayway in 2015 and has been employed as a cook at various cafés and restaurants for twenty-eight years. Customers look forward to her daily specials: Cuban rice and *gandules* (green peas) every Tuesday; meatballs with linguini and marinara sauce every Wednesday; taco bowls every Thursday; and at least one homemade soup every day.

By 6:30 a.m., pancakes, eggs and potatoes filled the flat-top grill, with more take-out orders streaming in by phone. Not long after Nuhem, Manny and Noel said goodbye, three guys from the Linden Department of Public Works, wearing reflective yellow vests, stopped in to pick up their orders. "Good morning, America," one of the workers joyfully proclaimed with arms raised. "Hey, I've missed you," another guy said to Jess. "Yeah, well, where have you been hiding?" she asked.

John Principato, known to the Linden faithful as "Johnny Prince," is the owner of the Bayway Diner. Principato, a fireman and the owner of a construction company, opened the place in September 2014. The previous owner, Mike Guinta, purchased the diner in October 2005 and, after doing some much-needed renovation work, had a successful run for about six years. The diner enjoyed a big splash of national media attention under Guinta's tour of duty. The Food Network's *Diners, Drive-Ins and Dives*, during the program's first season and eleventh episode, which initially aired on July 23, 2007, featured a segment on the Bayway. During a subsequent episode, show host Guy Fieri did a follow-up interview with Guinta and learned that the diner's popularity had exploded following the 2007 broadcast, as diner aficionados from as far away as Minnesota, Florida and California came to visit the joint. Guinta decided to focus on a separate business, Bayway Catering, and shuttered the diner.

Like other Linden locals, Johnny Prince enjoyed stopping at the diner but confessed that he always had his eye on buying the business. In addition to his skills as a fireman and mason, Principato said his experience in the food business goes back to his days as a teenager, when he worked at a Linden bagel shop. "I unlocked the front door in the morning and hand-rolled bagels." After graduating from Linden High School in 1983, he worked with his father, also a fireman, at a luncheonette on Elizabeth Avenue for nearly thirty years. It was there that the two firefighters developed their recipe for the Bayway Diner's signature dish: the famous Johnny Prince chili dogs.

"The food business comes naturally to me," Principato said. "It's in my blood. I love to see people enjoying good food and having a good time. It's more of a calling. I've put a lot of work into this place. I live in Linden. I came here for breakfast and lunch as a fireman, so I know how important the diner is to people in town and the truck drivers who stop here. This is my happy place."

ANOTHER HAPPY PLACE FOR truck drivers can be found fourteen miles north of Linden. The Truck Stop Diner, adjacent to the New Jersey Truck Stop complex, is a refueling station for man and machine located on Kearny Point, a spit of land nestled in between Newark and Jersey City, which sits in the shadow of the three-and-a-half-mile Pulaski Skyway.

Located on Routes 1 and 9—a congested, intense, unforgiving corridor that connects with the New Jersey Turnpike and leads to the Port Elizabeth and Port Newark marine terminals—the Truck Stop Diner, along with the New Jersey Truck Stop, is a haven for big-rig, intermodal trucks. "The truckers that come here are from Texas, California, the Carolinas, all over," said Stella, the head waitress. "They're all good people. After a while you

Truck Stop Diner. *Photo by M. Gabriele.*

become like a family. When they stop here, they bring us little souvenirs from around the country."

Caesar, the man who opens and closes the nearby Hackensack River Bridge, sat at the counter in late September 2018 and proudly proclaimed that he's been a loyal customer at the diner for forty-one years. "It's convenient," he said. "The people are good and so is the food." What's his favorite dish? "I order fried calamari for lunch every Friday."

Stella said that, by far, the best seller at the diner is the roasted chicken platter. Other big movers are *bistec encebollado* (Spanish steak and onions), meatloaf, stuffed peppers and oxtail stew served over beans and rice.

According to information posted on its website, the Truck Stop Diner, built by Kullman, originally was located in New York City and moved to Kearny Point in 1948. Sam Kolokithas and his family have owned the diner since 1989. Sam's son, Mike Kolokithas, is assuming managerial duties. "I was born in this place," he said. "It's a tough business, but this is a special diner."

# Not Much Has Changed

Anthony Musarra's quest to reconnect with the old White Crystal Diner from Atlantic Highlands represents a cross-country journey measuring many hundreds of miles and more than thirty years. A chapter in *The History of Diners in New Jersey* told the story of the White Crystal, owned and operated by the Natale family for forty years. Musarra, employed at the diner as a teenager during the 1980s, learned the value of making and saving money and gained insights on life and business from the regulars who frequented the diner.

The White Crystal closed in October 2000, and three years later, it landed in Cleveland, acquired by master diner rebuilder Steve Harwin and his Diversified Diners business. Harwin renovated the structure, originally built by Kullman, and sold it to restaurateur Vinnie Altier of Canton, Michigan. Altier, on January 1, 2012, reopened the diner from Atlantic Highlands as Vinnie's Hamburger Stand, located on Michigan Avenue (Route 12) in Canton. Today, it's known as Angie's Hamburger Stand.

Musarra relocated to New Mexico in 2008 but returns to the Garden State with his spouse, Valkyrie, to visit family. In May 2017, they embarked on a road trip to Michigan that included a stop in Canton to see Musarra's

Valkyrie Musarra at the rebuilt White Crystal Diner, now in Canton, Michigan. *Courtesy Anthony Musarra.*

old diner. He said they were warmly received by Altier and described the excursion as a sentimental journey. "It was a fun trip." How much had the diner changed? "Not much," he said, adding that it still has its fifteen stools and a long counter, staying true to its original layout—an interior design that sparks friendly interaction among patrons. The eatery maintains a classic diner menu: burgers, cheeseburgers, chili, fries, milkshakes and malts, root beer floats, chicken sliders, grilled cheese sandwiches, onion rings and coffee.

While he enjoyed seeing the diner, Musarra said his meeting with Altier turned out to be the real highlight of the visit. The two men—a Jersey guy and a Michigan guy—hit it off quite well. "Vinnie loved hearing about my stories of the diner back in the Atlantic Highlands days. He said it was his lifelong dream to own a 'real' New Jersey diner." When eating at a diner, "food is only half the meal," Vinnie explained during a 2011 phone interview. The other half is the diner experience—the patrons, the wait staff and the personality of the place. Musarra said goodbye to Vinnie, reassured that his beloved diner was reborn and in good hands.

# Blogging through a State that Isn't Boring

Cyd Katz, a 2004 graduate of Manalapan High School, is a dedicated blogger and creator of the travel and tourism website New Jersey Isn't Boring (http://newjerseyisntboring.com). She has visited and reviewed more than 250 Garden State diners since she launched the online venture in March 2014 and doesn't plan to stop anytime soon.

As spelled out on her website, Katz's goal is to inform residents and visitors about the Garden State's cultural attractions and seasonal events. Her areas of interest include diners, food trucks, craft beer, wineries and arts and entertainment. Her blogs offer a quick review of diners throughout the state. She said that while New Jersey diners are diverse and distinctive, there's a common thread: they reflect local pride. "It has a lot to do with the spirit of the community."

Katz values the fresh, homemade quality of classic diner fare, but she's especially pleased when she stumbles on something out of the ordinary. For example, in November 2017 she visited the Vegas Diner in Wildwood and enjoyed Boston cream pie pancakes, complete with custard filling and topped with chocolate. "When I placed my order, my waitress's eyes lit up

Vegas Diner. *Photo by M. Gabriele.*

and she told me I made an excellent choice," she wrote in her 2017 blog. "Generally, when I get a big, desserty meal like this, I end up eating half and taking the rest home, but not that day. It was so much food, but it was so delicious I couldn't stop eating it. I also skipped lunch. This meal has made it into my top-ten diner meals of all time."

Kelly Lindheimer (The History Girl, www.thehistorygirl.com) writes blogs about historic sites she visits throughout the Garden State, posting information and images on her website and Facebook page. The thrust behind her journeys is to provide "a better understanding and appreciation of New Jersey's history," which includes occasional stops at diners. Another blogger, freelance writer Kristen Koennemann (Only in New Jersey, www. onlyinyourstate.com), shares details of the many wonders to be discovered throughout the Garden State—diners, historic villages, outdoor festivals and nature sites.

## Before and After the Deluge

The history of the Bound Brook Diner is a saga of survival and relocation, which includes multiple name changes, locations, owners and even a historic flood. Through it all, the steadfast little diner kept finding a home and has stayed alive for seventy years.

The Cranford Theatre Diner, built by Fodero, opened its doors in downtown Cranford on Saturday, October 8, 1949. Its name was a reference to the popular Cranford Movie Theatre, which opened in the early 1920s. (The Cranford Theater Diner shouldn't be confused with the Cranford Diner—a separate eatery that operated in Cranford during this same period.) Charles and Grace Malpere owned the diner. The *Cranford Citizen and Chronicle*, on page one of its July 7, 1949 edition, reported that the Cranford Township Committee issued a construction permit to Malpere. The diner, in the building application, was given a value of $10,000.

Located at 101 North Avenue West, the Theatre Diner measured sixteen feet wide and forty feet long and had an overall seating capacity of forty-three people at the counter and booths. The Malperes built a separate structure that housed the diner's kitchen and restrooms. The *Citizen and Chronicle* wrote that the new eatery, "representing the latest in stainless steel diners," would employ eleven people and would be open twenty-four hours a day, seven days a week. The story pointed out that the Malperes had extensive experience in the diner business, operating a separate diner on South Avenue in Cranford for more than twenty years, as well as the Universal Diner in Morristown. They also owned Malpere's Restaurant in Summit.

In March 1957, the Malperes sold the Theater Diner to George Psak and John Danko. Danko, prior to working in the diner business, had served as a chef at New York State hotels for more than twenty years. April 1, 1957, was the grand reopening date for the Theater Diner in Cranford, now "under new management," as reported by the *Citizen and Chronicle*.

Judge George Psak Jr. said that his dad, George, who was born in Horna, Czechoslovakia, in 1926, served as an army sergeant in the Pacific during World War II. Psak said his parents originally resided in Bayonne but then relocated to Bound Brook when his dad and Danko became business partners. They planned to move the Theatre Diner to Bound Brook from Cranford, which would replace an existing eatery, which George Jr. described as a lunch wagon. Their plans to move the diner were put into motion, and on June 6, 1958, the Cranford Theatre Diner relocated to 502 East Main Street in downtown Bound Brook.

Frank Ryan, a former Bound Brook mayor, recalled the diner's arrival. As a lad growing up in Bound Brook during the 1930s and 1940s, Ryan's

Cranford Theatre Diner. *Courtesy George Psak Jr.*

117

most important daily chore was to deliver milk to the Bound Brook lunch wagon from the family's dairy farm. Interviewed in December 2017, Ryan said that his parents, Walter and Anna, owned the dairy farm (Ryan's Dairy) and the lunch wagon. He said the "new" Bound Brook Diner, relocated from Cranford, occupied the same footprint as the old lunch wagon. A 1950 graduate of Bound Brook High School, Ryan served in the navy from 1951 to 1955 and was elected as Bound Brook's mayor in 1999. He died on April 6, 2018.

The Danko and Psak partnership flourished, and Judge George Psak Jr. smiled when he recalled the days when he and his family worked at the Bound Brook Diner. "At age nine I wore a bow tie and helped my mom [Doris] at the cash register," he said. "I got a promotion. I became a dish washer and was very happy." George Jr. said his dad did much of the cooking at the diner and was especially fond of the morning shift. His father had a strong sense of community service and was a member of the Lions and Elks Clubs, preparing many fundraiser breakfasts for those organizations. George Sr. also was a generous man with a big heart. "My father never turned away anyone [in need] who came to the diner's back door," George Jr. said, adding that he showed respect to those less fortunate. "My dad took care of them. He gave them a small job to do and then gave them food."

Business at the Bound Brook Diner continued on an upward track, so much so that Danko and Psak confidently expanded their reach and acquired the Sunset Diner, which was located at 335 Route 22 in Green Brook, a neighbor to Bound Brook. Different iterations of the Sunset Diner had been at this location since the late 1920s. The Sunset, purchased by Psak and Danko, was a sparkling O'Mahony car, complete with an angled, mirror-image "SUNSET" sign complemented by a tall vertical "DINER" sign. The diner celebrated its grand opening under the new ownership on February 7, 1963. A four-column display ad graced that day's edition of the *Courier-News*, in which the new owners reminded readers that "we also serve you at the Bound Brook Diner." The Sunset Diner built by O'Mahony, under the previous ownership of John Riccardi, originally opened in Green Brook on October 8, 1940.

The arrangement for the business partnership involved George Sr. at the helm of the Sunset Diner, with Danko managing the Bound Brook Diner. George Jr., who did short-order cook work at the Sunset, said his lasting memory of the diner involved tour bus after tour bus stopping at the eatery, filled with people on their way to the New York World's Fair, which opened on April 22, 1964. The pace in the kitchen was fast

Sunset Diner. *Courtesy George Psak Jr.*

to accommodate the tour bus customers; French toast orders were in high demand. Paul Psak, George Jr.'s brother, was the main chef at the Sunset and also did much of the baking.

The Sunset Diner suffered a fire on Monday, June 7, 1965. The June 10, 1965 edition of the *Middlesex Chronicle* reported that the blaze caused extensive damage to the roof and partition between the kitchen and dining areas, with considerable smoke and water damage throughout the diner. George Jr. said this was a traumatic blow to the Psak/Danko partnership, but good will in the diner community saved the day. The food and service vendors that did business with the Sunset and Bound Brook diners came to the rescue, lending the partners money so they could stabilize their finances and rebuild. Joe Swingle, New Jersey's well-respected diner "renaissance man" and the leader of Swingle Diner Manufacturing in Middlesex, also pitched in and put a fast-track on constructing another Sunset Diner. The new Sunset Diner, built by Swingle, opened in mid-1966.

The Elik family purchased the Bound Brook Diner in the late 1960s. Danko and Psak sold Sunset Diner to John Logothetis and Nick

Koumarianos in January 1978. The Sunset Diner, under new ownership, continues to operate today on Route 22. George Jr. went off to study at Villanova University, where he had a roommate named Bill Smith, who later became known as Mustache Bill, with a landmark diner in Barnegat Light on Long Beach Island.

John Danko retired, and George Sr. turned his attention to the real estate business in central New Jersey. George Psak Sr. died on July 2, 2010; he was predeceased by his wife, Doris (Prusaksowki), who passed away in 2006. George Jr. described his mom as "the friendly face of the [Sunset] diner who greeted every customer on a first-name basis." According to information posted in his obituary, George Sr. was a three-time president of the Bound Brook Lions Club and the president and honorary "Man of the Year" of the Polish American Cultural Endeavors Association. George Psak Jr. entered the legal profession and enjoyed a distinguished career as a civil trial attorney and municipal judge and later became the supervising judge of Workers Compensation for Hunterdon, Somerset and Warren Counties.

The Bound Brook Diner continued as a popular eatery and enjoyed a shot of publicity when its stylish interior—red-and-white tile and stainless steel fixtures—was displayed on the cover of the 1996 book *Jersey Diners* by Peter Genovese. The diner also gained a share of cinema fame when, in June 1999, it appeared in a scene in the movie *Black-Eyed Susan*, a drama/murder mystery directed by Jersey-born Jim Riffel. While scenes of the movie were being shot at the diner, the *Courier-News*, in its June 14, 1999 edition, reported that owner Risto Elik was seeking to sell the diner and reviewing offers from potential buyers, including some from out of state.

The town of Bound Brook settled in for the easy tempo of summer days. People made plans to go "Down the Shore." Committees formed and campaigns were organized in preparation for municipal elections slated for later that year.

And then came the flood.

HURRICANE FLOYD BARRELED THROUGH the Garden State on September 16, 1999, dropping more than fourteen inches of rain. Information posted on the website www.njweather.org reported that Bound Brook, pinched by the confluence of the Raritan River and Green Brook, was inundated with fourteen feet of water above flood-stage levels. Businesses were swamped in downtown Bound Brook, including the Bound Brook Diner. The flood caused an estimated $100 million in damage in Bound Brook, according to news reports.

In the aftermath, Somerset County Surrogate Frank Bruno said that four feet of water and several inches of mud had collected inside the diner, but despite the damage the structure basically remained intact. Bruno, the president of the Bound Brook City Council at the time of the flood, had purchased the diner from the Elik family following the flood. In June 2001, Bruno had the diner wrapped in tarp and moved it to a storage facility in Bridgewater, saying that he intended to save it and find a new owner.

"The flood was a major catastrophe for us," Bruno recalled. "I loved the diner. I'm a diner fanatic. I wanted to save it as an icon. I didn't want it to leave Somerset County." However, one by one, potential deals to sell the eatery fell through. "I was under a lot of pressure. This was a sensitive issue in town. The diner had to have an owner with a viable business plan."

Bruno became emotional when asked why he went through the trouble of trying to salvage the diner. Growing up in Edison during the 1950s, Bruno and his dad, also named Frank, frequented the Baltimore Diner in New Brunswick. Built by Paramount, the Baltimore Diner, which was located at the intersection of Route 1 and Plainfield Avenue, celebrated its grand opening on February 22, 1942. "It was an amazing thing to go to a diner with my dad when I was young. I loved the atmosphere and the people we would see." In particular, he was in awe of "being surrounded by race car drivers that ate at the diner. These were *men*," he said, referring to the drivers, with a note of drama in his voice. Many drivers competed at the Old Bridge Stadium Speedway (1953–68), a half-mile paved track for modified stock car racing and drag racing. Bruno said his dad was a big race car fan and knew that the Baltimore Diner was a favorite spot for the drivers.

As he became discouraged and endured assorted tribulations in his attempts to sell the Bound Brook Diner, Bruno had no idea that the wounded eatery had a secret admirer—someone who would, quite literally, carry the diner to another state and the next chapter in its history. Bruno was contacted by Matt King, who grew up in Lyndhurst, where he worked as a teenager at San Carlo Restaurant. King graduated from Rutgers University in 1992. King originally had ambitions to become a history teacher but changed course, fell in love with the food business and became a restaurateur, working at franchises in Texas. King moved to Charlotte, North Carolina, in 2001 and managed a bagel franchise, but he had ambitions to open his own business. Relying on his Garden State roots, he had hopes of introducing a Jersey diner concept to the Charlotte region.

Baltimore Diner. *From the collection of Larry Cultrera.*

According to an online article posted by Charlotte's WSOC TV news, King and his partner, Steve Estes, in 2001, read a story in a local paper that opined that unless Charlotte was home to a "real" twenty-four-hour restaurant, it never would be considered "a real" metropolitan city. "The two [King and Estes] had spent their careers managing popular restaurants for other people, and were more than ready to start one of their own," the story stated.

King said that by the end of 2001 he had "put pen to paper" and began drafting a detailed business plan, enlisting potential investors and weighing locations. It was during this time that he stumbled on his *Jersey Diners* book, with the cover photo of the Bound Brook Diner's interior. Something clicked. He was smitten and quietly began a determined search to locate this diner.

After a number of months, King connected with Bruno, and the two men negotiated the sale of the diner. King's family and friends, aware of the diner's condition, expressed their doubts. "You got to be crazy," King said, recalling the feedback that he received from friends. "I knew the diner had its problems, but I saw beyond all that. I said, 'Don't worry, we'll fix it.'" Finally, King and Bruno reached an accord, and in June 2005, the diner embarked on a six-hundred-mile journey via flat-bed tractor trailer truck to North Carolina. For Bruno, the transaction was a bittersweet moment.

Bound Brook Diner. *Courtesy Al Beronio.*

"It broke my heart," he confessed. Though relieved that he had fulfilled his mission to save the diner, "The sad part is that it left New Jersey."

King and his colleagues worked on restoring the diner for several years. Finally, the well-traveled eatery, now known as Mattie's Diner, opened on Friday, August 6, 2010, in an Uptown Charlotte district known as the "Music Factory" entertainment complex. Almost immediately, the diner became a festive scene, especially after concerts, with customers lining up outside the door and waiting for spots at the seventy-seat outdoor patio. Along with music fans, the diner also attracted members of classic car clubs, civic organizations, neighborhood regulars and a fair share of curious tourists. King, describing himself as a "hands-on" diner owner who works the grill, said that he and his staff were well prepared for the hungry, enthusiastic throng, pumping out milkshakes, burgers, fries, sandwiches, egg platters, fried chicken and waffles, "drunken" onion rings, fried beer-batter Jalapeno peppers, grits and livermush. *Livermush?* "It's comparable to corned beef hash in New Jersey," King explained. "It's delicious."

A May 5, 2009 episode of the TV program *Bizarre Foods with Andrew Zimmern* did a segment in Shelby, North Carolina, the livermush capital of the United States. Zimmern interviewed locals during the town's annual livermush festival, held in mid-October, and learned that livermush is a blend of pork parts—liver, fat, skin and the hog's head. It's processed by adding corn meal and spices and then baked into a loaf, similar to the consistency of liverwurst. Most often it's sliced into patties, deep fried and then served on a roll with condiments that include mustard, mayonnaise or grape jelly. The local delicacy first became popular during the Civil War and then was rediscovered during the Great Depression years.

King said that his customer base in North Carolina already had an affinity for fresh, down-home food, "so there was not that much education we needed to do in terms of introducing the diner culture." The region, he said, has numerous family-friendly "country kitchen" establishments that have similarities to diners. He added that Charlotte, as a growing business center, has lured many New Jersey residents during the last ten years. "People loved the diner," King said, saying he had no concerns about the diner establishing an identity. "We had lots of customer interaction. At a restaurant, the owners worry about creating an atmosphere. At a diner, the customers create the atmosphere."

After five lucrative years, change once again came to the diner from New Jersey. King said that in the fall of 2015, a new owner purchased the Music Factory property with plans to build an office complex. Unable to afford the property on which the diner sat, and faced with the dilemma of being forced to close, King networked through his sources and received an offer to relocate from private real estate investment company RJS Properties, to be a featured attraction in a greenway business district, about three miles from the Music Factory site. Because of the proximity to his former location, King is confident that the social media buzz will help him retain many of his loyal customers. (A deal to relocate the diner had not yet been finalized as of July 2019.)

King remains a man on a mission. He became nostalgic when thinking about his carefree younger days when he and his friends ate at the Lyndhurst Diner, the Colonial Diner (in Lyndhurst) and the Tick Tock Diner. "Going to those diners was part of growing up when I was growing up."

Asked what keeps him motivated to overcome business challenges, King paused for an existential moment to take a deep breath and then chuckled and spoke from the heart. "This is my personality," he said, referring to his discipline and drive to pursue his goals. "It's part of my family and who I am. I always wanted my own place; something that Charlotte needed and that I needed. I fell in love with this diner and the idea of bringing it to North Carolina. I love to cook at the grill and I love my customers. It's been a good living and I've made money. The diner is something special. It's part of us. When people walk in for the first time and see it, they understand that we're saving a piece of history."

# The Other Diner in Cranford

As mentioned earlier, the Cranford Theater Diner and the Cranford Diner were two separate eateries in the Union County town. The October 23, 1924 edition of the *Cranford Citizen and Chronicle* carried a small two-column ad for the Cranford Lunch Wagon, operated by Louis Billias and Harry Chronas and located at 7 North Avenue in downtown Cranford. Presumably, the business had another owner prior to Billias and Chronas, as the ad stated that the wagon was "under new management" and "open day and night."

The first lunch wagon served the community from 1923 to 1928. It was replaced by a larger lunch wagon, which operated from 1928 to 1942. Chronas left the business in 1936, and Billias carried on alone. In 1942, a diner was installed at the North Avenue site, and seven years later, Louis Billias retired, leaving the business to his sons, Pete and Nick.

A new Cranford Diner, a structure built by O'Mahony, opened at the North Avenue site on Wednesday, February 18, 1953. The diner had a seating capacity of one hundred customers and measured sixty-five feet by seventeen feet. The newspaper, in its February 12, 1953 edition, carried two left/right facing full-page ads (pages four and five) to herald the new

Cranford Diner, circa 1949. *Courtesy Vic Bary, Cranford Historical Society.*

ANOTHER FORTY YEARS

Peter Ganiris, Sherban's Diner. *Photo by M. Gabriele.*

Peter Ganiris, the convivial owner of Sherban's Diner, reminisced about how he was born on the Greek island of Chios and came to America at the age of sixteen. Ganiris then recounted the classic New Jersey entrepreneurial diner tale: he started as a dishwasher and saved his money, and through hard work and determination he ended up owning the South Plainfield establishment, which he has operated with great pride for more than forty years. Alex Sherban, the original owner of Sherban's Diner, launched the business in the late 1950s. Born in America, Sherban's family originally came from Romania. "Alex was a good guy and proud of his business," Ganiris said. In 1972, Ganiris and John Stellakas acquired the diner from Sherban, and three years later, they installed a new diner on the site, manufactured by Swingle. The two partners expanded the diner in the 1980s, adding a dining room and a larger kitchen. Several years later, Ganiris bought out Stellakas. He joyfully proclaimed that he plans to run the business for another forty years.

diner's grand opening. "The Cranford Diner is pleased to offer residents of Cranford and vicinity the very finest in diner service," the grand opening ad read. "In our new diner, you may enjoy the finest foods, prepared in our spotless stainless steel kitchen and dine in beautiful air-conditioned comfort." The eatery served Arborn's Coffee from a roaster based in Linden, and there were three broilers in the kitchen. "We are fully equipped to cater to large parties, weddings, and receptions." Among the diner's amenities, there were "automatic hand dryers in rest rooms for sanitary purposes."

On the facing page, fourteen businesses, all of whom provided services or supplied food for the new diner, offered congratulations. Diner manufacturer Jerry O'Mahony was most notable among the well-wishers. "We built it [the diner] and our wish to you is that you have continued success," the ad read.

In April 1965, the Billias family announced that it had sold the diner to John Flangoes and Angelo Nokas. Following some minor renovation work, the diner reopened one month later. John Priovolos, who owned the popular Lido Diner, located on Route 22 in Springfield, purchased the Cranford Diner in 1975. It evolved into the Downtown Family Restaurant and Diner, still at the same 7 North Avenue address. Priovolos ran the business until 1986, when he leased it to a new management team. After three years, he returned to the eatery and ran it with his daughter, Tina Priovolos. John Priovolos died on May 25, 2016, and Tina kept the business going until announcing it would close on June 1, 2018. The *Union News Daily*, in an online article posted June 9, 2018, wrote that the regular customers turned out to say goodbye to Tina.

# SOUTHERN NEW JERSEY

## It All Depends on Where You Live

Diner fans throughout the Garden State were anxious to hear President Barack Obama address a controversial topic during his May 15, 2016 commencement speech at Rutgers University. The following is an excerpt of his remarks, as dutifully recorded by the White House Office of the Press Secretary:

> *I come here for a simple reason, to finally settle this Pork Roll versus Taylor Ham question. I'm just kidding. There's not much I'm afraid to take on in my final year of office, but I know better than to get in the middle of that debate.*

It's Pork Roll in southern half of the state and Taylor Ham in northern half. The mystical dividing line runs through East Brunswick. Call it what you like, it's all Jersey and all good—and a favorite among diner goers. John Taylor, born in Hamilton Square on October 6, 1836, is credited as the creator of the product. As a homegrown New Jersey delicacy and diner staple, it consists of smoked processed pork and spices.

The 1907 book *Genealogical and Personal Memorial of Mercer County, New Jersey* noted that Taylor originally was employed in a brick yard owned by his father, James F. Taylor. James Taylor died when John was just fourteen years

Taylor Ham/Pork Roll, egg and cheese on a roll (to go). *Photo by M. Gabriele.*

old. Taylor continued to work at the brick yard for three more years and then worked for a retail grocery store, Rainear, Son and Company, for another three years. He then withdrew from that business and formed a partnership in another retail grocery store with a man named James Ronan. At this point, Taylor was twenty years old and the year was 1856—the year sources cite as the creation of Taylor's Pork Roll recipe. It's more than plausible that the young, ambitious John Taylor "invented" Pork Roll during this period. Considering his line of work, he certainly would have been familiar with salt curing and the processing of meat products. An August 2015 profile of John Taylor by historian Richard Sauers, posted on the Riverview Cemetery blogspot, and an article in the February 11, 1909 edition of the *Trenton Evening Times* both concurred with the chain of events given in the 1907 book for Taylor's early career.

After two years, Taylor bought out Ronan's share of the business. The 1910 Mercer County genealogical book reported that "in 1860 [John] Taylor associated himself with D.P. Forst in the wholesale grocery business, and such partnership continued until 1870, when Mr. Taylor sold his interest to Mr. Forst. About this date, Mr. Taylor engaged in the pork packing and cattle business on quite an extensive scale. This was really the foundation of the present Taylor Provision Company. The Taylor Provision Company of Trenton, of which Mr. Taylor is president, was organized in 1888 and is regarded as among the most important commercial interests of the city."

George Washington Case developed a competing recipe for hickory-smoked Pork Roll in 1870. He originally sold pork roll from his farm in Belle Mead. The family business, Case's Pork Roll Company, spans six generations and is based in Trenton, according to the company's website.

Jenna Pizzi, author of the 2015 book *The Pork Roll Cookbook*, pointed out (in a lighthearted way) that despite the differences in north/sound lingo, Pork Roll is technically the correct name for the product. (Regarding food definitions, "pork" refers to meat from any part of a pig, while "ham" specifically refers to meat from the pig's thigh or rump.) "People are fanatical about their love for this product," Pizzi said, when asked to sum up the "take away" on her research for the Pork Roll book. She feels a sense of comradery with that enthusiasm. "Pork Roll has a long history and has withstood the test of time. It's profound that people have such a connection with [a food product that's] so mysterious. It makes me love New Jersey even more." She prefers her Pork Roll with an egg over easy and a slice of white American cheese on a Kaiser roll. (The question of whether to use white or yellow cheese is another controversial topic.)

Pizzi grew up in Moorestown and currently resides in Philadelphia. During her days as a reporter for the *Trenton Times*, Pizzi covered the first Pork Roll Festival, which was held on May 24, 2014, on South Broad Street in Trenton, a lively gathering that attracted thousands of fans.

In her book, Pizzi wrote that the Taylor Provision Company churned out the cured pork treat, which John Taylor referred to as "Taylor Ham." His son, William, eventually took over the family business. "In 1906, the Federal Meat Inspection Act was passed, regulating the slaughter of animals, the processing of meat and, more importantly to Taylor, requiring the exact labeling of all meat and meat food products. Taylor proudly peddled the name Taylor Ham, which was problematic because the product was pork, not ham. Rebranding as Pork Roll didn't hurt business," Pizzi wrote.

Some of the Pork Roll/Taylor Ham name conundrum also can be traced to an early twentieth-century legal case (*Taylor Provision Co. v. Gobel*, Circuit Court, E.D., New York, August 15, 1910, "Action by the Taylor Provision Company against Adolph Gobel for Trademark Infringement."). Pizzi explained that the court ruled against Taylor Provision's complaint, saying the term "Pork Roll" was considered a basic product description and couldn't be trademarked. Questions over packaging also were part of the case. According to the trial transcript, found in the 1910 book *The Federal Reporter*, volume 180, the court found that:

> *Where the complainant's* [Taylor Provision] *evidence did not show that the words "Pork Roll" as used by him, or "Taylor's Pork Roll," in connection with the sale of pork in cylindrical cotton packages, had acquired a distinct meaning in the eyes of the public for the particular article of food described before* [the] *defendant put his product on the market in similar packages, complainant was not entitled to a preliminary injunction to restrain defendant's use of such packages and dressing….The motion will be denied.*

A supporter of the Republican Party, John Taylor was elected state senator for Mercer County in 1880. He died on February 10, 1909, at the age of seventy-two and was buried at Trenton's Riverview Cemetery. The *Trenton Evening Times* covered the story on page one of its February 11, 1909 edition and praised Taylor in an editorial as "a self-made man of humble birth" and a philanthropist who promoted the greater good. "For years he was prominent in every public enterprise for the betterment of the city [Trenton]….Mr. Taylor never forgot his own early struggles and was ever sympathetic toward young men who were seeking to better their fortunes. With sound business and political judgment, generously charitable, progressive and public spirited, he was a good and useful citizen."

Taylor's biggest gift to Trenton was the Taylor Opera House, which opened on March 18, 1867, and was torn down in 1969. And his biggest gift to New Jersey's diner culture was…well, you know, that tasty processed meat product you eat on a Kaiser roll paired with an egg over easy and a slice of American cheese.

# "Don't Stand Behind Me"

He is, quite simply, the gold standard in New Jersey's illustrious diner business—a diner man's diner man. He even has a James Beard Award to prove it, along with a track record of more than forty-five years and hundreds of loyal, satisfied customers.

Watching Bill Smith perform at his namesake Mustache Bill's Diner in Barnegat Light on Long Beach Island is seeing a grand master at

Bill Smith. *Photo by M. Gabriele.*

the top of his game. He's an intense bundle of coiled energy, moving with precision at high speed in an enlightened state of consciousness, instinctively collecting ingredients needed to prepare meals on the flat-top grill. Bespectacled and sporting a funky bandana, he twists, turns and whirls in the kitchen wielding his spatulas. Fair warning is given to his kitchen associates through words written on the back of his Mustache Bill's T-shirt: "Don't Stand Behind Me."

"I was an army brat," Bill said during an impromptu, in-kitchen interview in August 2018. (As I asked questions, I kept a safe distance as he folded omelets and flipped pancakes.) "My dad [also named Bill Smith] retired from the army, and we settled in this area when I was eleven years old." A 1969 graduate of Southern Regional High School in Stafford Township, Bill recalled working as a dishwasher at the diner as a teenager in the mid-1960s. The diner, built by Fodero, originally opened on May 9, 1959, as the New Barnegat Light Diner, as reported by the *Beach Haven Times.* Joe Sprague, who previously owned the Beach Haven Diner, also on Long Beach Island, was the original proprietor. Following the May 9 grand opening, the diner offered a special Sunday Mother's Day turkey platter for one dollar.

Bill Smith, the father, suffered a heart attack when young Bill was in his third year at Villanova University. "I left Villanova for a while to be with him,"

Bill said. "The diner became available in 1972, and it was my dad's idea to buy the place." Originally dubbed Bill's Barnegat Light Diner, Bill recalled that "some local wise guy, who was interviewed for an article on Long Beach Island in the *Sunday New York Times* travel section in 1976, kept referring to us as 'Mustache Bill's Diner.'" The wise guy–inspired moniker stuck, and the Long Beach Island locals began to call the place "Mustache Bill's." As a result, moved by popular consent, Bill renamed the diner accordingly.

The diner's cheery atmosphere is maintained by the friendly wait staff, led by good guy and concierge Ken Meredith, Bill's best friend since fourth grade. "This is the place where people get together to talk and have a good meal," Ken observed. "We have groups of the same four or five people who show up here every week." Bill's sister, Dottie, works in the kitchen. The diner eatery continues to shine, as it has withstood storms and the salty Atlantic Ocean breezes for sixty years. Along with the legendary Cyclops—a fried egg set into the middle of a pancake—the menu includes egg platters, soups, burgers, salads, club sandwiches and "catch of the day" fish dishes.

Bill Smith acquired his cooking skills by coming up through the ranks of the diner business. "Bill's self-taught," Ken confirmed. "He learned on the job. He's the real deal." Part of his apprenticeship came in 1970, when he worked at the Sunset Diner in Green Brook, alongside his Villanova

Mustache Bill's Diner. *Photo by M. Gabriele.*

roommate, George Psak, whose father owned the Bound Brook and Sunset Diners. Bill's dad died in 1981, and part of his father's legacy at the diner is a Pennsylvania-style recipe for chipped beef.

The 2009 James Beard Foundation Award, named in honor of the great American chef, author and TV personality (1903–1985), is proudly hung on the dining room wall in a display case:

> *For more than thirty-five years Bill Smith has made everything for scratch, refusing to buy anything pre-made. It's the homemade, straight-from-the-heart cooking that makes Mustache Bill's a must-stop destination on the Jersey Shore for the fishing community, regulars and the summertime beach goers.*

# Dining Among the Many Deer

More than eight thousand miles separate the Garden State's sacred Pine Barrens and India's Goa State. This is the distance that represents Manny Monteiro's journey, which unfolded over a number of years and with several ports of call, to become the owner of a New Jersey diner. Today, traveling south on Route 206 through Burlington County, motoring along the lush, pastoral woodlands, intrepid diner fans will come to "the place of many deer," the translation of the Native American word for the village known as Shamong, the home of Manny's Shamong Diner.

Manny hails from Goa State, located on the country's western coast along the Arabian Sea. He grew up in a rural environment—fishing villages and towns with limited access to electricity and running water. After graduating from Little Flower of Jesus, a Catholic high school, in 1977, Manny initially had ambitions to become a mechanic or possibly an engineer, but he also showed a secondary interest in cooking. He said his homeland once was a Portuguese colony, with a local food culture that mixes European and Indian/Hindu influences.

Following advice from his brother, Manny began attending culinary schools in western India and then went to Kuwait, where he spent several years doing food service work for hospitals as well as hotels and hostels. He also met Alice Augustine, his bride-to-be. Alice had designs on pursuing her career as a registered nurse in the United States and had an invitation from a cousin to relocate to Cherry Hill. Alice and Manny landed in New Jersey in 1988, and Manny's extensive résumé allowed him to continue his career

*Left*: Manny and Alice Monteiro at the Shamong Diner. *Photo by M. Gabriele.*

*Below*: Thali platter at the Shamong Diner. *Photo by M. Gabriele.*

in institutional cooking in Philadelphia and western New Jersey while Alice became a nurse.

In the mid-1990s, Manny became the food service director at YMCA Camp Ockanickon in Medford. Besides his position at the camp, Manny also worked as a realtor. In 2006, he learned that the Shamong Diner was for sale and purchased it. He always wanted his own business, and the opportunity appealed to him because it was a small diner, not a large restaurant, and had a choice location on Route 206. Manny had a business strategy that would capitalize on his international culinary skills. He would differentiate the Shamong Diner in this neck of the Jersey woods by offering vegetarian and Indian cuisine along with standard diner fare.

A serious businessman who takes pride in his skills as a restaurateur, Manny has joyfully immersed himself in Jersey culture. "I've met the most amazing people at the diner," Manny said. "My customers look out for me. They've learned to trust me and they're open to try something new."

A delicious supper at the diner in early September 2017 began with a bowl of smooth, savory butternut squash soup. The main course was a Thali vegetarian platter, a royal sampler of jasmine rice, Chana masala (curry chickpeas), Aloo Gobi (cauliflower and potatoes), Dhal (lentils), Raita (yogurt salad with crunchy fruit slices), naan (Indian bread) and rice pudding. Each selection was a delicacy. Manny mixes his own Indian spices. In 2013, he added a pizza oven to his kitchen.

# A West Virginia Girl Lands at "The Coin"

Carolyn Spano, during the early 1980s, became a Sunday morning regular at the Silver Coin Diner, located on the White Horse Pike in Hammonton. "I'm a West Virginia girl, so I really enjoyed the cream chipped beef and biscuits that they served." After coming to the place once a week for nearly a year and consuming multiple orders of her favorite dish, one of the owners, the late Gus Tzaferos, approached her. Gus realized Carolyn was a familiar face and wanted to engage in some small talk. Gus and his brother, George, purchased the Scaffidi's New Colonial Diner in 1981 and christened it the Silver Coin the following year, so they made efforts to build good relationships with customers.

The conversation between Carolyn and Gus was cordial enough, but she wasn't about to let a good opportunity slip away. She seized the moment: "I told him that I've been coming to the diner for a year and I enjoy the food,

Carolyn Spano at the Silver Coin Diner. *Photo by M. Gabriele.*

so I really think it's about time that you offer me a job," she declared. Gus's eyes lit up, and he didn't miss a beat. "Can you start tomorrow?" he asked. Carolyn joined the Silver Coin as a waitress in 1983.

After many years of working long hours as a member of the diner's wait staff, Carolyn currently serves as a hostess and cashier for the Silver Coin. She smiled and provided her job description: "I welcome you, I seat you and when you've finished eating I take your money."

Driving north on Route 54, where hypnotic, late-afternoon mirages glimmer in the roadway like ghostly pools of water, the Silver Coin emerges out of the Pine Barrens as a sparkling, colorful outpost. The United Diner Company of Philadelphia did the construction work to expand and renovate the old colonial-style diner. Menu items include daily specials such as grilled pork tenderloin marinated in olive oil, lemon juice and Greek spices; broiled sockeye salmon; slow-braised Yankee pot roast; Alaskan codfish crusted with potatoes, chives and cheddar cheese; and chili lime tilapia.

For New Jersey diner fans who enjoy indulging in a rich source of antioxidants and micronutrients through the consumption of blueberry pancakes, blueberry pie and fresh blueberries on their waffles, please note that Hammonton takes pride as the Blueberry Capital of the World, the hub of the Garden State's yearly harvest of nearly 60 million pounds of blueberries, with the majority of that total coming from Atlantic County, according to an April 2016 online article posted by NJ.com.

Carolyn said that her career in the diner business began when, as a teenager, she was a waitress at the Penrose Diner in South Philadelphia. Carolyn was born in West Virginia, where her father was a coal miner. In the mid-1950s, Carolyn's uncle, recently discharged from the army, contacted her dad and told him that there was good construction work to be had in Willingboro Township. This was the time and place when the Garden State's version of Levittown was being built—a huge residential development by Abraham Levitt and Sons, according to the website Levittown Beyond. The first home in New Jersey's Levittown development was occupied in October 1958. Spano's dad came to New Jersey and sent for the family once he secured his job in Levittown. Several years later, Carolyn relocated to Philadelphia but then returned to New Jersey and lived in Williamstown, just a short hop from the Silver Coin.

A keen observer on the southern New Jersey diner scene for more than thirty-five years, Carolyn said that her favorite shift as a waitress at the Silver Coin was 11:00 p.m. to 7:00 a.m. "Absolutely," she said, as she recalled the cavalcade of entertaining characters that stumbled through the doors during the graveyard hours. The Atlantic County eatery is located at the confluence of Routes 206, 54 and 30—a trio of roadways that connect the diner to a diverse regional customer base. Carolyn said that every two hours during this late shift she would greet and serve distinct waves of patrons. It began when Hammonton-area state troopers and bartenders started arriving just after 2:00 a.m. Famished, bleary-eyed Atlantic City gamblers poured in between 4:00 a.m. and 5:00 a.m. (this was the period when the casinos were required to close for a two-hour stretch every night). Farmers, fishermen and truck drivers would show up between 5:00 a.m. and 6:00 a.m.

"It's a pleasure to go to work. Every day is like a family reunion. I enjoy talking to people. I love to hear about their families and their careers." She said her most memorable customer was John Halliday, who served as

Silver Coin Diner. *Photo by M. Gabriele.*

a captain for New Jersey State Police. Carolyn said he first arrived at the diner as "a newbie," and she came to know him during his career in law enforcement, where he specialized in crime scene forensic investigations. He retired in January 2012 after twenty years of service as a trooper. What made Halliday so special? "I don't know, we just hit it off as friends," she said. "He used to come in late at night for take-out orders. He was very polite and friendly; the sweetest thing on two feet." She took him under her wing and counseled Halliday on his dietary needs. "When he walked in, I would take one look at him and say, 'John, this is what you need to order today.'"

In a separate phone interview, John Halliday remembered the day when he first met Carolyn: it was lunch at the Silver Coin on January 27, 1986. Three days earlier, the twenty-year-old Halliday had become a member of the 103rd class of New Jersey State Troopers, fulfilling a childhood dream. Meals at "The Coin," as Halliday calls it, were a tradition for Troop A (southern New Jersey) officers. "She was a sweetheart," he said of Carolyn, adding that the owners, brothers George and Gus Tzaferos, and diner staff members went out of their way to accommodate the troopers and make them feel comfortable.

The diner served as refuge for the troopers, with a good meal or a cup of coffee breaking the tension of their day. Halliday spent sixteen years in Troop A and then was promoted to captain and finished his career at the State Trooper Division in West Trenton. A trooper's professional life involves long, intense, stressful hours. Halliday said that when working on a crime scene investigation, he and his fellow troopers sometimes would go for two days straight without a break, running on adrenalin and determination. "The Coin was our rallying point," he said. "We would work crazy hours, but when we were done, we'd all go to the Coin. That was our reward. Thinking about the Coin is what kept us going."

## Just Because You Can Doesn't Mean You Should

After contemplating the passage of time, people and cars along Route 9 for more than twenty-five years from his vantage point at the Forked River Diner, Robert Moody, on a Sunday morning in April 2017, was more than pleased to share his philosophy of life and the secret of running a successful diner. "Pay your bills on time and be happy about it," he said with a grin.

Robert and Nancy Moody are the owners of the diner, which is located in its namesake town of Forked River. "People call me Moody—just Moody," Robert said. "Yeah, you got that right," one satisfied customer chimed in. Moody said he and Nancy took over the business more than a quarter of a century ago after Nancy's parents ran the place for eight years. Prior to Nancy's parents, it previously was known as Ray's Diner. It's no accident that the diner's original look and charm have remained intact, as Nancy and Moody have worked hard to preserve it.

The mustachioed Moody said the diner attracts a large contingent of fishermen and weekend boaters, drawn by the satisfying food and superb coffee. Most customers and the wait staff converse on a first-name basis. The eye-catching exterior architectural feature of the Forked River is a big-brim, wrap-around awning. The highlight color of the exterior panels is teal, which is repeated throughout the interior, complemented by a green speckled terrazzo floor with golden diamond patterns. Kullman manufactured the Forked River at its Harrison facility, circa 1953.

The special dish on that Sunday morning in April was the Chunky Monkey Pancakes—golden-brown flapjacks generously loaded with bananas and chocolate chips, plus a side order of bacon. I order two

Forked River Diner. *Photo by M. Gabriele.*

pancakes, but my waitress Kassandra encouraged me to spring for a taller stack. "Just two?," she asked, with a twinkle in her eye, hoping I would up the ante. "I bet you could eat seventeen." I told her I might be able to eat seventeen, but when gauging the proper amount of food to consume at a diner in a single session, a wise rule of thumb to follow is: just because you can doesn't mean you should.

# The Halfway Point

Joseph A. DeMarco worked at the Ford Motor Company plant in Chester, Pennsylvania, during the 1930s and 1940s, assembling cars and then building tanks during World War II. One day in 1945, he surprised his family by driving home in a new Ford, presumably just off the assembly line in Chester. Unfortunately, following the end of the war effort, DeMarco unexpectedly was laid off from the Ford plant, which operated from 1927 to 1961. Refusing to be deflated by the unlucky turn of events, he hatched a new idea and drove off one day in August 1946. Once again he surprised his family, this time by returning home with a used car and an announcement that he sold the new Ford and used the money to help him purchase a diner.

A typewritten contract dated August 24, 1946, and provided by DeMarco's daughter, Kitty, stated that DeMarco bought the Hearth Diner, a Silk City car built by the Paterson Vehicle Company, which was located at 2310 Broadway (adjacent to a shipyard) in Camden, for $12,500. DeMarco made arrangements to have the diner moved to a piece of property he owned in Hammonton along the White Horse Pike (Route 30) and opened the diner in November 1946. DeMarco named his establishment the Midway Diner, as it marked the halfway point between Philadelphia and Atlantic City on the White Horse Pike (Route 30). Before the opening of the Atlantic City Expressway in 1965, summertime beachgoers from the Philadelphia area used Route 30 as a primary roadway to reach Atlantic City.

Kitty recalled that her dad grew up in Hammonton, operated a gas station and had a knack for fixing motors. DeMarco also knew his way around a kitchen and grill, having acquired cooking skills by osmosis while growing up in his Italian family, with ancestral roots in Naples, Italy.

As a 24/7 eatery, the Midway became a popular spot during the late 1940s and into the 1950s, especially among the fashionable Atlantic City nightlife crowd. Famous professional sports icons, such as heavyweight boxing champion Jersey Joe Walcott and New York Yankees star Joe DiMaggio, frequented the Midway Diner. DeMarco, in 1953, purchased an O'Mahony diner to replace the Silk City car. He expanded the kitchen and opened a cocktail lounge to suit the tastes of the Atlantic City glitterati.

Kitty said that her dad hired skillful chefs, bakers and line cooks from New York City, all of whom contributed to the Midway menu with daily specials of Spanish, German and Italian dishes, along with homemade pies, cakes and donuts. The diner's coffee, a special blend created by the Ireland Coffee Company of Atlantic City, drew raves. A legendary purveyor and regional roaster of coffee found throughout the Jersey Shore, Samuel W. Ireland had established the company in 1917, initially roasting coffee beans for Atlantic City hotels, according to a March 17, 1996 article in the *New York Times*.

The star of the Midway was a waitress known to the customers as "Blondie"; her real name was Cecila Bonnette. Blondie spoke with a sultry southern accent, knew her business and didn't take guff from anyone. She became a mentor for Kitty, who worked as a waitress and also did the bookkeeping for her dad.

Joseph DeMarco died in 1955 on the day after Christmas. His brother, John, who owned a produce distribution company, took over ownership of the diner. Among the many people expressing condolences to the family, Kitty's mom, Pauline, received a handwritten letter, postmarked December 28, 1955, from Enoch L. Johnson, the legendary Atlantic City political boss. "Dear Mrs. DeMarco, I am very sorry to hear the sad news about your husband, who was a fine man and who will be greatly missed by his many friends. At this time let me extend my sincere sympathy to you and other members of the family. Regret very much I cannot attend the services because of a broken leg. With kind regards, sincerely, Enoch L. Johnson."

The HBO TV series *Boardwalk Empire* fictionalized Johnson's life and career. Known as "Nucky," he dominated Atlantic City politics from 1913 to 1941 and died in December 1968, according to several online sources. While he's portrayed as an infamous character in the TV series, Kitty said that many people in the Atlantic City region saw Johnson as a benevolent figure. "He [Johnson] used to stop at the diner," Kitty recalled. "He and my father became business acquaintances. He respected my dad."

The DeMarco family continued to operate the Midway until selling the business in 1973. The new owners ran it for another five years, until finally shutting down the diner. After sitting idle for a number of years, the diner property was converted to the Midway Professional Center in the 1990s, as

## Over Easy in Egg Harbor City

Egg Harbor City in the 1920s and 1930s was home to two early diners. Joe's Diner, owned by Joseph Molasso and established in 1921, was located at Sixth Terrace and the White Horse Pike. The Ideal Grill, owned by World War I veteran Charles Kuehnle, opened on January 26, 1929, and originally was located on the White Horse Pike at the corner of Fifth Terrace. Molasso died on January 26, 1939, due to injuries he suffered in an auto accident. Joe's Diner was removed and replaced by a second iteration of the Ideal Diner in 1940. That diner later relocated to Pomona and then was shipped to Europe. The present-day Harbor Diner, located at 613 White Horse Pike (Route 30) at the corner of Sixth Terrace, occupies the spot held by the previous diners. Tax records indicate that the Harbor Diner was built in 1967 and has since been remodeled.

Joe's Diner, Egg Harbor City. *Courtesy Mark W. Maxwell, Egg Harbor City Historical Society.*

Harbor Diner. *Photo by M. Gabriele.*

reported in the March 21, 2018 edition of the *Hammonton Gazette*. The same article reported that the old diner site along White Horse Pike, which included an abandoned gas station, was cleared to make way for a "Super Wawa" convenience store.

# The Best Calf Roper in New Jersey

It was nearly high noon when Bob Roberto sauntered into the Swedesboro Diner one sunny day in early June 2018, wearing his ivory-colored Resistol-brand cowboy hat, his leather cowboy boots and his heavyweight silver and gold belt buckle—an impressive keepsake that celebrates his 1983 calf-roping championship at Madison Square Garden, New York. Born in 1947, Roberto grew up in the Passaic County town of Haskell. Roberto won calf-roping championships throughout the United States, and in between his numerous competitions, he enjoyed good food, conversation and relaxation at many a diner.

Roberto is a Jersey guy, a diner aficionado and a cowboy who's recognized by fans whenever he attends shows the Cowtown Rodeo in Pilesgrove Township, Salem County, which was established in 1929 and is one of the oldest American rodeos. Roberto won seven calf-roping championships at Cowtown, where he's considered a living legend.

Diners have been an integral part of his life as a rodeo cowboy ever since he was seven years old, when he first starting learning from his father, Carmen, how to rope a calf and ride a horse. At age seven, after he attended a rodeo at Madison Square Garden with his dad and his dad's friends, they dropped in at midnight at the old Golden Star Diner, located on westbound Route 46 in Little Falls (today the site of the Park West Diner). That night, young Bobby learned a strict lifelong lesson from his father about not wasting food and wanting what you order. "After that night, I always made sure I cleared my plate," Roberto said. He entered his first competition at age eleven at the rodeo in Englishtown, riding his horse Outlaw. He tied for third place and won twenty-six dollars.

During his teenage years in Haskell, Roberto said that he and his high school buddies spent lots of time eating and socializing at Guide's Diner, where he enjoyed the diner's homemade ravioli dinners. He ticked off an extensive list of favorite Garden State diners he has visited during his years of cowboy wanderings: Blairstown Diner; Woodstown Diner (not far from

*Above*: Bob Roberto's rodeo belt buckle. *Photo by M. Gabriele.*

*Left*: Bob Roberto at the Swedesboro Diner. *Photo by M. Gabriele.*

Cowtown); the Lyndhurst Diner; Pals Diner; and Paul's Diner, which was located in Secaucus on Route 3 on the edge of the Meadowlands. "That was a real good one," he said of Paul's. Today, the Swedesboro Diner is his favorite. "I get a discount as a senior citizen, and the chicken Francese melts in your mouth."

For thirty years, Roberto and his dad were diner buddies as they toured the country and "rodeoed" together. Meal conversations between son and father were snippets of cowboy stories. He entered nineteen rodeo competitions per year, from California to Maine, from Florida to Wisconsin. "Rodeos usually start at 7:00 p.m., and you can't eat before the competition [due to the demanding physical activity involved in calf roping]. When we were done, it was after 10:00 p.m. and we were hungry. A diner is *the* place to stop for a meal because the food is good, the prices are reasonable, they have a big menu, and they're open late at night. You can get anything you want." As for favorite dishes, Roberto often went for the special of the day (turkey, chicken or roast beef), while his dad preferred seafood. They usually skipped dessert, unless the waitress informed them there was an especially good pie that day.

Carmen Roberto passed away in 1992. Today, Bob Roberto lives in Gloucester County, still owns horses, visits his friends and fans at the Cowtown Rodeo and enjoys watching his son, Troy, compete as a calf roper. And although he's still a diner fan, he lamented how much things have changed on the road over the years. "My dad and I used to drive from New Jersey to Florida and we could get a home-cooked meal anywhere we stopped. Not anymore. Today, it's all fast-food places. When we were traveling, we would go to our favorite diners and see people we knew and waitresses that worked there for years. Today, everyone has a cellphone, but no one is really connected. This is part of Americana that we've lost."

# A Birthday Cake for Liberace

During the mid-1970s, driving west on Route 70 at 5:00 a.m. in his 1976 Ford Pinto, Chris Corvasce felt the pressure and pinch as a medical school student. He was headed toward the Ben Franklin Bridge and Philadelphia during those predawn hours, enrolled at Hahnemann Medical School (today part of Drexel University). The pressure came from his rigorous studies and long hours working at hospitals. The pinch came from his wallet, short on disposable income.

Most of his meals those days consisted of bland hospital cafeteria food. As a modest splurge to lift his spirits and break the tension of his grueling schedule, Corvasce—a 1971 graduate of Nutley High School—found solace at the counter of Olga's Diner, located in Marlton. Once a week, he budgeted $1.25 for a slice of blueberry pie and a cup of coffee at Olga's.

"That was my treat," he said. "Olga's was a great diner." Sustained by pie and coffee at Olga's, Corvasce went on to become board certified in internal medicine and gastroenterology.

According to online news stories and social media postings, the origins of Olga's, owned by the Stavros family, date back to a diner in Camden in the mid-1940s, located at Sixteenth and Federal Streets. John Stavros named the diner in honor of his mother. The Camden diner did well, but by the late 1950s, Stavros had determined that the time had come to relocate the business. He eyed a location in Marlton, "because that was the one place where Routes 70 and 73 intersected," Steve Stavros explained, on behalf of his father, John, during a January 2018 phone interview. He said those two roadways became popular with tourists and vacationers in the Philadelphia area looking for a direct passage to the Jersey Shore. A 2012 book by John S. Flack Jr., *Evesham Township* (Images of America), noted that the two roads were planned in the late 1920s. They ran through

Evesham in the 1930s and were widened in the early 1940s. It was during this period that the Marlton Circle opened, marking the confluence of these two roads.

A deed dated October 28, 1959, provided by Evesham Township via an "open public records act request form," documented the purchase of property on the Marlton Circle by the Stavros family. Steve Stavros said that at the time of the purchase, the region surrounding the traffic circle consisted of apple orchards, dairy farms and corn fields, but his father envisioned the location as having great potential for a diner. John Stavros selected Fodero to build the dazzling new Olga's Diner. Marlton resident Walt Evans, who worked at a gas station on the Marlton Circle, watched the deliveries of exterior panels and kitchen equipment as the diner was being built. "We never saw anything like it before," Evans said.

Stavros said that the diner opened its doors in April 1960. Flack wrote that the diner expanded in 1965 with a large bakery and extra dining rooms to accommodate up to four hundred patrons. Olga's bakery endures as the most delicious memory of the diner, a remembrance expressed during casual conversations with Marlton-area baby boomers. Local residents unashamedly swoon with any mention of the cheesecake, pastries, cream pies and fruit pies produced by the diner's bakery.

Acclaim for the diner grew as a steady stream of cars filled Routes 70 and 73 and development came to the Marlton area. Along with motorists, truck drivers and tourists, there was one other source of business for Olga's: patrons from the Latin Casino, a popular night club in nearby Cherry Hill. *South Jersey Magazine*, in its July 2014 edition, and an online article posted June 2, 2015 by the *Daily Journal* provided information on the entertainment venue. Originally based in Philadelphia, the Latin Casino opened in Cherry Hill in late 1960, coinciding with the launch of Olga's. "The Latin" had more than two thousand seats and featured stellar performers such as Frank Sinatra, Nat King Cole, Ella Fitzgerald, Sammy Davis Jr. and the pianist Liberace. The Latin closed in 1978 due to financial difficulties and the rise of Atlantic City casinos. The *Journal* article reported that the club briefly reemerged as the Emerald City Disco, but the structure was torn down in December 1982.

Olga's attracted celebrities and fans from The Latin as the late-night place to go after the show. Steve Stravros said that (Wladziu Valentino) Liberace became a loyal patron and friend of the diner, so much so that Olga's bakery, as a creative gesture of appreciation, outdid itself with a piano-shaped birthday cake for its famous customer. In turn, he said that

Olga's Diner. *Photo by M. Gabriele.*

Liberace (1919–87) graciously provided a framed, autographed photo to the diner in 1973, which was proudly put on display.

Legions of customers continued to support Olga's during the next thirty-five years, but in 2008, Olga's Diner encountered a string of difficulties that involved disagreements with local officials over utility charges and tax issues, according to newspaper reports. The diner suffered periodic closings until it shut down for good in December 2008. In 2009, the state initiated plans to reconfigure the Marlton Circle with overpasses. Steve Stravros said that his family ultimately prevailed in the disputes with municipal officials.

An online column posted on July 31, 2013, on Philly.com recalled the state of affairs. "Olga's Diner, a landmark that once attracted hordes of travelers [on their way] to the Jersey Shore, was shuttered five years ago," Jan Hefler wrote. "We said our goodbyes then, but its skeleton and eight-foot red neon sign remained, a nod to the past. Then, when the Marlton Circle was removed during a highway improvement project, the old building became an island surrounded by traffic at the crossroads of Routes 73 and 70. Now, Olga's Diner has been declared 'blighted' and all traces of it could soon be condemned and demolished. The Evesham Township Council deems it an eyesore. Goodbye again old girl." Hefler's observations were on target. Demolition crews began to raze the structure in June 2017; five months later, all traces of the diner had disappeared.

Newspaper articles in September and October 2018 reported on plans to build a new Olga's Diner on Route 73 in Marlton—a venture that doesn't involve the Stavros family. An online story noted that the Evesham Township planning board had approved the plan in the spring of 2018 and that the new owners broke ground on October 2 for the $3 million project. Other online news reports in June 2019 indicated that construction work was underway and making progress.

# Geets

A ribbon-cutting ceremony on March 24, 2018, celebrated the reopening of Geets, a landmark diner located at the intersection of Route 322 (the Black Horse Pike), Route 42 and Sicklerville Road in Williamstown. Entrepreneur Sandy Cannon of Franklin Township, who has fond memories of going to Geets during her formative years (cream of chicken soup every Sunday was a family tradition), purchased the property through federal bankruptcy court in January 2017, a transaction valued at $3.9 million.

A self-described "Jersey Girl," Sandy—whose business holdings include a bridge painting company, a real estate investment firm and a farm with fifty-two cows—saw the diner as an intriguing opportunity. In acquiring the property, she pledged to Monroe Township officials that she wouldn't demolish the diner. Instead, she decided to rehabilitate and maintain the structure. The diner required significant capital investment to install a new kitchen, a new roof and a rebuilt foundation, along with upgraded plumbing and electrical systems. She also made a point of preserving the familiar, vertical "GEETS" sign that faces the Black Horse Pike.

Sandy and her husband, James, put together a team and a strategy, and rebuilding work began in March 2017. "I've never owned a diner or a restaurant, so it was kind of scary," she said.

Amid the excitement of the diner's rebirth, Kathryn Rose Sylvester Fletcher shared her family's memories on the history and origins of Geets. Her grandfather Francis Sylvester worked as a cook at a restaurant in Glassboro beginning in 1932. "Geets" was an affectionate family nickname for Francis. He and his wife, Rose, had a dream of owning their own diner. After working for more than twenty years, they used their life savings for a

Geets Diner. *Photo by M. Gabriele.*

down payment in a lease/purchase agreement for a diner known as Cooper's Restaurant, located at the site of today's Geets. They opened the business on March 13, 1953. The original white, masonry building had a rounded front entrance and a rectangular dining area. The property included an adjacent, smaller "twin" building—a Mobil gas station. Kathryn said that the diner, which showcased a pinball machine and juke box, had a seating capacity of fifty, which included a counter with ten stools.

As anticipated by her grandparents, the population in the Williamstown area began to rise, which generated more business for the diner. After three years, Francis and Rose decided to invest in a new diner from Fodero. They entered into a contract agreement, beginning with a payment of $675 in a note dated March 12, 1956—the first of forty-six scheduled payments. Kathryn's dad, Frank, joined his parents in running the diner. Business continued to increase, and in the early 1960s, the family expanded the dining room and added a banquet hall. Kathryn's mom, Ann Sylvester, did the bookkeeping and worked the cash register during busy holidays while raising five children. Fodero, in 1969, built a new Geets Diner. There were additional expansions and redesigns throughout the 1970s and 1980s. Kathryn said that liver, bluefish, stuffed flounder, meatloaf, steak sandwiches, bread pudding and rice pudding were favorite items on the menu.

On April 10, 1987, the Sylvester family sold Geets Diner to a partnership that lasted for one year. "Another entity came in, with my father holding the mortgage, which was paid off eleven years later," Kathryn said. By 1997, the Sylvester family was completely out of the diner business. Geets continued to operate under a series of owners until it closed abruptly on August 1, 2016, according to newspaper reports. News articles also indicated that the diner's ownership, which initially had filed for Chapter 11 bankruptcy protection, later changed that status to Chapter 7 liquidation. As mentioned earlier, six months later Sandy purchased the property through bankruptcy court.

Today, Kathryn is an attorney living in Connecticut, and she's happy that the Geets legacy continues with new ownership. During her teen years, her duties at the diner included cashiering, washing dishes, peeling potatoes and waitressing. "I'm very proud of my family," Kathryn said, underlining her Italian ancestry. "Diners are significant because they're really about community. They're places for business meetings, after-church meals, dates, birthdays and a coffee break from the day's challenges."

The diner experience continues to have a profound impact on Kathryn's life:

*After my dad sold the business, I continued to work in diners during the summer and on school breaks through college, graduate school and law school. I still know how to lift two trays full of dishes and how to stack plates in my arms. My kids say I'm a big tipper, even when the service is bad. Sometimes I have to resist the mad urge to pour my own coffee or get up and clear a table when some overwhelmed waitress is in the weeds. Working in the diner taught me how to talk to complete strangers about anything; how to move and make decisions quickly; how to make people feel at ease; how to read people; how food should be prepared; and how to keep working even when you're physically exhausted.*

# Dewey's Note

Homer Felknor and his buddies would drop in at the Holly Diner after high school to drink soda and listen to the jukebox. The sound of rock-and-roll was in the air, and teenagers were tuning in. "We all liked rock-and-roll, but Elvis wasn't my favorite, at least not until I found out how much the girls like him," Felknor said. The diner's interior had a long counter that fed into a dining area, which provided ample floor space for teenagers to dance.

Felknor's mom, Reba, ran the diner in the early 1950s, having spent a number of years working as a waitress at various eateries in southern New Jersey. Felknor's dad, also named Homer, a chief warrant officer for the army, made the financial arrangements for his wife to operate the Holly Diner. "Most likely it was some sort of lease agreement," Felknor said. After more than two years, his parents tired of the business, its long hours, maintenance expenses and related headaches, and they left the diner.

Growing up in the Burlington County town, which sits on the western edge of the Pine Barrens, Felknor graduated from Rancocas Valley Regional High School in 1956 and then joined the U.S. Air Force. Since those days, he's traveled extensively and now lives in Oklahoma, with a home in Florida for the winter months. These days, he rarely visits Mount Holly but maintains vivid memories of the diner. A fifty-cent breakfast special of eggs, steak, potatoes and coffee reigned as the diner's most popular dish, day or night. Each day, his mom and her line cooks prepared a Blue Plate special and soup. The diner sat at the intersection of Mill and Pine Streets in downtown Mount Holly, adjacent to an Acme Supermarket, Gottlieb's butcher shop and a Sinclair gas station. Felknor said that during the 1940s and 1950s, Mount Holly prospered as a community, with its local economy boosted by the Eagle Dye textile mill and the presence of the Fort Dix military base, located just ten miles away.

Felknor recalled two frequent visitors at the diner. The first, G. Mathis (Matt) Sleeper, the editor of the *Burlington County Herald* newspaper, showed up at various times throughout the day, along with a staff photographer, to drink multiple cups of coffee and "sniff out stories around town." The second was a homeless man who went by the name Indian Joe. Felknor said Indian Joe lived in an abandoned shed outside of town. He showed up at the diner to do odd jobs like sweep the floor and dispose of the trash. Reba paid him and gave him a hot meal. "She never turned him away," Felknor said. "Mount Holly was a small town. Everyone knew everyone, so we took care of our own." Residents also enjoyed the Madison Diner.

The Mount Holly Diner, originally known as the Hollybrook Diner, was another favorite spot for Mount Holly teenagers in the 1950s and 1960s. Located at the intersection of Route 38 and Pine Street, the Mount Holly Diner celebrated its grand opening, under new management and ownership, on March 31, 1960. A display advertisement in the *Mount Holly Herald* invited customers to visit the diner for the grand opening, stating there would be "free coffee and gifts to all."

One man, posting a remembrance on the "Mt. Holly Area, Yesterday and Today" Facebook page, recalled his teenage years at the diner through the magic of haunting rock-and-roll harmonies. "I remember sitting at a booth, mesmerized, hearing the Everly Brothers sing 'Cathy's Clown' for the first time on the jukebox." Other Facebook posts focused on a waitress named "Dewey." She was a lifelong Mount Holly resident and a 1958 graduate of Rancocas Valley High School. "The Mount Holly Diner was a nightly visit for me as a police officer. It got me started," one man wrote. "One of the highlights was a waitress by the name of Dewey. She could always put a smile on your face." Other page members said that Dewey "was always doing something for others. She is missed by many. She was a beautiful person and friend."

One person with a lasting memory of Dewey is Jim Wengert. "We stopped there nightly for coffee, cheese fries, and burgers. Dewey, with her flaming red hair, had a great personality and was one of the funniest people I have ever met." Wengert joined the Marine Corps, and prior to shipping out to Vietnam (he served there from 1969 to 1970), he stopped at the diner to say goodbye to Dewey. "She gave me a guest check and wrote a note on it that said: 'Bring this back to me for a free coffee.' I stuck it in my wallet, and that check was with me at Quang Tri, Phu Bai and Marble Mountain and Da Nang. Fortunately I came home, but I never did cash in my check for coffee. I still have it somewhere."

Dorothy A. "Dewey" Rockwell died on April 12, 2010, at the age of sixty-nine.

Wengert's note from Dewey kept him connected to his hometown during his tour of duty in Vietnam. Maybe it's best that he never did cash in the note for a cup of coffee. It remains a living memory and a keepsake from a waitress with red hair who worked the night shift, was a dear friend to many in Mount Holly and could always put a smile on your face.

*Photo by M. Gabriele.*

# Starlight Dancing in Giampietro Park

What came first—the chicken, the egg or Vineland?

Vineland came first, and then thousands and thousands of eggs laid by hundreds and hundreds of chickens at Vineland hen houses. According to an article published in the January 1883 edition of the *Poultry Monthly* magazine and information provided by the Vineland Antiquarian and Historical Society, Vineland in 1882 (just twenty-one years after Charles Kline Landis founded the community), shipped 208,000 eggs to distribution markets in New York and Philadelphia. Jewish immigrants, many from southern Russia, established poultry farms in Vineland, as reported in the December 29, 1975 edition of the *New York Times*. John T. Cunningham, in his book *This Is New Jersey*, wrote:

> *The founding of the Vineland Cooperative Egg Auction in 1931 focused attention on the chicken farmers in the northeastern section of Cumberland County. The auction sold more than $50 million worth of eggs in its first twenty years and claimed to be the largest egg cooperative in the world. Vineland called itself "the egg basket of the nation."*

It's a safe bet that many of those delicious Vineland eggs were gently carried through food industry distribution channels and consumed by diner patrons in the Garden State and elsewhere. Patricia Martinelli, administrator of the Vineland Antiquarian and Historical Society, said that by the 1950s, the Vineland and the surrounding region supported more than 250 poultry farms. The *Times*, in the same 1975 article, estimated that Garden State egg production peaked in the mid-1950s. There also was a parallel egg cooperative in Flemington. An online article posted on September 7, 2016, at nj.com reported that the Flemington organization produced 450,000 cases of eggs in 1955. Several news articles indicated that by the mid-1970s, the cooperatives in Vineland and Flemington were shuttered and had ceased operations.

Landis's vision of Vineland as a progressive, temperance (alcohol-free) community in Cumberland County, laid out in a precise street grid, was more than a vague dream. Throughout the late 1800s, Vineland became a magnet for business and innovation. In addition to egg production, there was an agricultural sector producing a bounty of vegetables and fruit grown by Italian immigrant farmers. Vineland also became home to textile, glass and iron industries; department stores; and shoe manufacturing.

The 2014 Postcard History Series book *Vineland* by Arjorie Moniodis Ingraham and the Vineland Historical and Antiquarian Society provided background information on Landis, an "ambitious" Philadelphia attorney and "a man who was both a devoted humanitarian and a staunch capitalist. Landis had been involved in real estate development, but he saw Vineland as a place where he could imprint his own beliefs. In this new 'village,' as the town originally was called, one's race or religion did not matter as much as respecting the rights of others, including women. In 1861 Landis bought about 20,000 acres from Richard Wood of nearby Millville. By the end of the [Civil] War, the town had become the home of scholars, business owners, inventors and artists." The book pointed out that Vineland became known as a progressive center for the women's suffrage movement and civil rights. The town inaugurated trolley service along Landis Avenue in August 1901, as part of its fortieth anniversary celebration, according to an article in the April 15, 2015 edition of the *Daily Journal.*

Diners were popular in Vineland against this backdrop of high-energy business and social consciousness. According to articles in the *Vineland Evening Times*, the first was Jennings Lunch, an eight-seat lunch wagon opened in 1915 by Frederick Mortimer (F.M.) Jennings, located at the intersection of Landis Avenue and Boulevard. By 1929, Jennings Lunch had expanded into a larger barrel-roof diner at the same location. Jennings died on January 4, 1939, and his nephew, John H. Bishop, took over the business. On November 1, 1941, Bishop opened a modern, "factory built" diner on the same site. The diner car measured forty-four feet long and seventeen feet wide and had a seating capacity of fifty-two, including twenty stools at the counter. The new eatery featured an extra-large kitchen for baking and stainless steel throughout its interior and exterior, with a light-green terrazzo floor.

Nucci's Diner, owned by brothers Les and Fred Nucci, a popular 24/7, air-conditioned diner built by Jerry O'Mahony, opened in July 1948 at 418 Landis Avenue, as reported in the July 20, 1948 edition of the *Vineland Daily Journal*. Nucci's was located adjacent to the old Grand Theater. In the late 1950s, the Nucci brothers retired, and Frank J. Martinelli and Frank Imburgia purchased the diner.

Nucci's continued to operate through the 1960s and 1970s and was torn down on June 22, 1992. The diner had been shuttered for more than ten years prior to the demolition. The *Daily Journal*, in a page-one story in its June 23, 1992 edition, described the diner as the unofficial

Landis Avenue Trolley, 1907, Vineland. *From the collection of M. Gabriele.*

center of Vineland politics and a favorite spot for late-night eats. One politician, quoted in the story, described Nucci's as "the place of the evening." A former city councilman said that it was neutral ground where local politicos could do away with formalities and "let down their hair. We'd talk and we'd argue." A third source said the diner was the place where Vineland's Democrats and Republicans would meet and negotiate. "Many important deals that helped perpetuate the city's growth were made there."

A column in the June 29, 1992 edition of the *Daily Journal* ("Millville, by George") reminisced about the passing of the diner:

> *As I was lamenting the recent demise of Nucci's Diner, the orchestra in my mind started playing a medley of songs…"The Way We Were," "Memories," "Those Old Familiar Places," "That Old Gang of Mine." The bulldozers have buried Nucci's, but not the memories. Nucci's* [was] *the place where every night out ended, the place to see and be seen, the place to hear and be heard. Nucci's* [was] *more than just a place, it was a state of mind. Late night breakfast, eggs over easy, sausage, home fries, coffee and another cigarette. Oh sure, the Nucci's we knew and loved has been nonexistent for a long time. But at least we could show the building to our*

*grandchildren and spin our tall tales. Will the coffee ever taste so good? Will the eggs, sausage and home fries ever be so flavorful? Will any place, anywhere, fill the void left by the departure of our favorite haunt? No! The orchestra plays one last tune, "Long Ago and Far Away."*

As detailed in articles by the *Daily Journal*, along with information from the Vineland Historical and Antiquarian Society, other diners in town included Joe's Diner, opened in 1936 by Italian immigrant Joe Meandro; the Publix Diner, which replaced an older diner at Sixth Street and Landis Avenue and opened June 22, 1940; and the Presidential Diner, which opened in 1969 and was renamed the Vineland Diner in March 1991. Today, Tony's Lunch and the Golden Palace carry on Vineland's diner tradition.

John "Junie" Quinesso, a World War II veteran and 1943 graduate of Vineland High School, said that his favorite spot in town was Jim and Larry's Diner. (The nickname Junie comes from his younger days, when his family often called him "Junior.") He went to the diner "always in the evening after a movie or a dance, and always for coffee." James Zaragosi and Larry Catti, two men with extensive experience in the business, opened the diner on July 7, 1949.

Quinesso served with the navy in the Pacific Theater—shuttling supplies between Pearl Harbor, Okinawa, Guam, Saipan and Wake Island—and returned to Vineland in 1946. In the spring of 1948, Quinesso stopped at the Sun Ray drugstore on Landis Avenue and noticed a pretty young woman named Rose Di Domenico working in the cosmetic department. "I asked her on a date and the rest is history." They married in 1950 and remained active on the Vineland social scene, going to the movies and local dances. Those outings usually included a stop at Jim and Larry's Diner. "The diner was a convenient place to go after a movie," he said. "It was a meeting place for the town. It was informal. You could go there to sit and chat with your friends or meet new people."

Life was good in Vineland for John and Rose during their forty-five years of marriage. Rose passed away on February 8, 1995. She worked as a secretary for the Vineland Board of Education and retired in 1983. "She was a lovely lady," Quinesso said, with sweet notes of admiration in his voice, perhaps picturing Rose the first time he saw her at the Sun Ray drugstore.

Interviewed in July 2018 at the age of ninety-two, Quinesso said that he often attends the free summertime Monday night concerts and dances at Giampietro Park in Vineland at the Enrico Serra band shell. One

John ("Junie") and Rose Quinesso. *Courtesy John Quinnesso.*

evening, in the summer of 2017, he was approached by a woman who looked familiar. "I remember you," she said to Quinesso. "My name is Frances and I worked at Jim and Larry's Diner. I used to wait on you and your wife." The two laughed and he described the reunion as a beautiful surprise, which allowed his memories of Rose and the diner to come alive. Today, Quinesso and Frances recall their diner days as they foxtrot under the stars at Giampietro Park.

# Let's Get to the Point

The *Atlantic City Press*, in its June 1, 1960 edition, reported on the ribbon-cutting ceremony for the Point Diner in the town of Somers Point. Dignitaries pictured in the newspaper photo for the diner's grand opening, held on May 31, 1960, included Joseph A. Montano and Herman Green, the top executives of United Diner Manufacturing Company, the Newark-based builder of the diner; Andrew E. Magill, owner of the Point Diner; and Fred W. Chapman, the mayor of Somers Point. The article said the $300,000 diner had a seating capacity for two hundred people and a parking lot that could accommodate three hundred cars. "[The diner] is decorated with flame-colored plastic booths with gold-flecked Formica table tops. Lighting fixtures are gleaming gold against a white ceiling background. The service areas are stainless steel. The main dining area is L-shaped and completely air conditioned."

In a previous article, the *Press* reported that there had been a smaller diner on the same site, which was sold and moved. United Diner began production of the Point Diner in October 1959. It was transported to Somers Point in six sections, including the vestibule, by flat-bed trucks. The kitchen and bakery

Point Diner. *Photo by M. Gabriele.*

were constructed on site. The diner, located on MacArthur Boulevard, has been remodeled and enlarged over the years.

A 1963 advertisement noted that the diner specialized in steaks and "ocean-fresh" seafood and had a "complete bakery for weddings, parties and special occasions." During the 1960s, late-night customers from Tony Mart's Rock and Roll nightclub, also located on Somers Point, flocked to the Point Diner.

# Heading Down the Shore to Have a Ball Once More

*Sleeping on the beach, seven days a week*
*Rocking every night, till the early bright*
*Whoa whoa whoa whoa those Wildwood days*
*Wild, wild Wildwood days*
*Every day's a holiday*
*And every night is a Saturday night*
*—"Wildwood Days," written by Dave Appell and Kal Mann;*
*performed and recorded by Bobby Rydell and released in May 1963*

Wildwood, the swinging Jersey Shore resort town, captured the youthful, boundless exuberance of rock-and-roll in the late 1950s and early 1960s. Hot rods paraded up and down the boulevards, beeping their horns. The flamboyant Doo Wop architecture of hotels and restaurants captured imaginations and provided a dreamy setting for the summer fun. Music, dancing, romance and party lights at Wildwood's music clubs—along with surf, sun and sand—attracted revelers from Philadelphia and throughout New Jersey. And all the while, sitting in the background to all this merriment, there was a diner scene well prepared to feed the masses when music clubs closed in the early morning hours. Fans engaged in all that high-energy rocking, burning off hundreds of calories each night, needed to refuel with burgers, French fries, pancakes, eggs, bacon and milkshakes.

Al Brannen, president of the Wildwood Historical Society Inc., which maintains the George F. Boyer Historical Museum, shared his memories of those years. Born in Philadelphia, Brannen grew up in Bucks County, Pennsylvania. At age nineteen, he enlisted in the U.S. Coast Guard and was

## SKINNY'S DINER

Local residents, Atlantic County politicians, entertainers and musicians passing through Atlantic City rubbed elbows as they enjoyed cups of coffee and quick meals any time of the day or night at the Hy Grade Diner, which was located at 34 North Main Street in Pleasantville. As reported in the *Mainland Journal*, the diner's first owner, Pete Fiori, opened the barrel-roof diner, and it soon became a landmark. "The diner came brand new from the factory in 1922—unloaded from a freight car." Frank Reiche, known as "Skinny," began working for Fiori in 1928 and then assumed ownership in April 1944. The diner closed in March 1972, and Reiche died on October 9 that same year. A bulldozer leveled the diner in mid-January 1973.

Hy Grade Diner. *Courtesy Nancy Caruso Bonner.*

stationed at Wildwood from 1961 to 1965. "The music clubs and bars let out at 3:00 p.m.," he said. "There were thousands of people in the streets." Many dropped in at Wildwood's diners for an early morning breakfast and then went to the beach to watch the sun rise. "It was chaos and craziness for a few hours, but it was good craziness," Brannen continued. "It was an exciting time, just like what Bobby Rydell sang—every night was like a Saturday night. A lot of young people from Philadelphia came to Wildwood. Music was the big thing."

Wildwood remained a popular shore resort and entertainment destination even as rock music went in different directions during the 1960s and into the 1970s, but then casino gambling opened in Atlantic City on Friday, May 26, 1978. The days of nonstop Saturday nights in Wildwood quickly faded away. "Things really changed when Atlantic City got gambling," he said. "It killed our nightlife and tourism."

An article in the September 4, 2005 edition of the *New York Times* provided a snapshot of this idyllic period. "From the early 1950s through the early 1970s, Wildwood rocked on a regular basis," the story stated. "Atlantic City, up the road about 30 miles, was the summer scene for a slightly older generation." Philadelphia disc jockey Ed Hurst, quoted in the story, explained that "the rock acts couldn't get booked in Atlantic City, so they looked for someplace else, and that was Wildwood."

The *Times* article also quoted several musicians from the period, spinning their stories of the wild Wildwood days. Drummer Dick Richards recalled that his group, the Comets, which featured a "cowboy singer" named Bill Haley, performed the hit "Rock Around the Clock" for the first time on Memorial Day 1954 at a club called the HofBrau, which was on Atlantic Avenue.

The *Press of Atlantic City*, in a July 2, 2014 feature story, stated that a talented eighteen-year-old musician named Ernest Evans—who was born in Spring Gulley, South Carolina, in 1941 and grew up in South Philadelphia—performed at the Rainbow Club in July 1960. He went by the stage name of Chubby Checker and introduced a cover of a song written and recorded a year earlier by Hank Ballard. "The Twist" became a major number-one hit sensation.

The article also stated that Wildwood became the preferred destination for Philly rock-and-roll teen idols Frankie Avalon, Fabian (Fabiano Anthony Forte) and Bobby Rydell, along with Dick Clark, the host of the TV show *American Bandstand*. Their favorite place in those days was the Wildwood Diner, located on Atlantic Avenue, between Young and Spencer

Avenues, which opened on May 27, 1955. The O'Mahony car had a center vestibule and large neon script letters ("Wildwood Diner") displayed on the eatery's rooftop. A full-page display ad in *The Leader* newspaper touted it as "Wildwood's newest and most modern air conditioned diner," open twenty-four hours a day. An article in the March 31, 1955 edition of the newspaper previewed the diner's arrival as a "$100,000 project" with a seating capacity of one hundred.

Owned by the Muziani and Scrocca families (Guy Muziani was a former Wildwood mayor), the Wildwood Diner unveiled an expansion on April 25, 1961, which included a large vestibule, added seating capacity, an exterior tower with a new neon diner sign and the diner's distinctive turquoise-colored exterior panels. The Superior Diner Manufacturing Corporation, based in Berlin, New Jersey, did the remodeling and expansion work.

Forty-five years later, the diner quite literally disappeared overnight. *The Leader*, in its Wednesday, August 9, 2006 edition, reported that the Wildwood Diner "went from landmark to barren land in forty-eight hours this week. A demolition crew arrived on Monday and by Tuesday there was little left but twisted steel and rubble. It was *the* late-night spot…during the city's Doo Wop heyday." The diner was razed to make way for a high-rise hotel. At the time, diner fans, city residents and local historians bemoaned the diner's demise as one of the more egregious examples of Wildwood losing an important piece of its history.

The Lamp Post Diner, located in North Wildwood and built by Paramount in 1947, was torn down on December 20, 2015, according to an online post by the Wildwood Video Archive. Angie and Lloyd's Hilltop Diner, located on East Oak Avenue, opened in 1958 and also was demolished.

THE FOURTH OF JULY is a day that holds a significant place in the family history of Michael John, the owner of the Surfside West Diner, located on New Jersey Avenue. It's part of a legacy that reflects Michael John's life as a successful Wildwood diner owner. On July 4, 1940, Michael's dad, Thomas Michael John Sr. ("Tomi"), who grew up in Bitoli, Macedonia, arrived in the United States with his family at the age of thirteen. On July 4, 1963, Tomi John opened the Surfside Restaurant. After running the business for more than thirty years, Tomi John passed away on July 4, 1994.

Interviewed in August 2018, Michael John, a member of the Wildwood High School class of 1972, said that his dad, along with several partners, opened the Surfside Restaurant, as previously mentioned, which was

## BACON AND EGGS IN THE PINE BARRENS

Nestled on Route 50 in the Pine Barrens, the Tuckahoe Family Diner is a South Jersey golden age survivor, a Silk City car built in the 1940s. According to a July 2009 *Press of Atlantic City* article, framed and displayed inside the diner, a flatbed truck deposited the eatery "in an empty Tuckahoe parking lot" (presumably where it currently sits) in 1956. Originally known as Robinette's Diner, it has changed ownership several times since the mid-1980s.

Tuckahoe Family Diner. *Photo by M. Gabriele.*

located in the Wildwood Crest section at the intersection of East Lavender Road and Ocean Avenue. The round structure with an extreme zig/zag roof line, built in the fanciful Doo Wop style, had a large awning over the main entrance, with a flamboyant aqua, orange and gold color scheme, according to notes in the "John Family History" (with text excerpted from the book *Wildwood by the Sea: Nostalgia and Recipes*). Michael John said that his dad also operated other restaurants and luncheonettes in the area during this mid-1960s period.

In the summer of 1994, three days after finalizing a deal to buy out his partners at the Surfside Restaurant, Tomi John died of a heart attack. Michael John and his wife, Jeanne, assumed ownership of the restaurant and ran it for eight years before deciding to sell the business in 2002. The distinctive Doo Wop restaurant was in jeopardy of being torn down, but a grass-roots movement of local residents, led by the Doo Wop Preservation League, purchased and saved the structure. It was disassembled, moved to its current location on Ocean Avenue, on the grounds of Fox Park and across the street from the Wildwoods Convention Center, and reborn as the Doo Wop Experience Museum, opening in June 2007.

After selling the Surfside Restaurant, Michael and Jeanne decided to purchase the Crestwood Diner, built in 1963 by Superior Diner and located at the intersection of Jersey Avenue and West Cresse Avenue. They remodeled the eatery and renamed it the Surfside West Diner, which opened on Mother's Day weekend (May 10 and 11), 2003. Michael John said that catering for local organizations, family parties and special events has become the growth segment of his business. The Surfside West menu offers customers house specialties such as green eggs and ham, with pesto sauce as the "green" component; lemon ricotta pancakes; Challah bread French toast; and "hangover" bowls—home fries, cheese and chipped beef topped with a fried egg.

The Vegas Diner (mentioned in the section "Blogging through a State that Isn't Boring") on New Jersey Avenue in North Wildwood opened in 1979. Remodeled in the Mediterranean style, with its red-tile roof and field stone exterior, the Vegas has won its share of "Best Diner" awards for Cape May County over the years. Other diners in Wildwood include the Doo

Surfside West Diner. *Photo by M. Gabriele.*

Pink Cadillac Diner. *Photo by M. Gabriele.*

Wop Diner (a storefront property on the boardwalk), the Seaside Diner, the Marvis Diner and the Star Diner and Café.

The Pink Cadillac Diner, located at the corner of Atlantic and Garfield Avenues, celebrates Wildwood's rock-and-roll heritage with a checkerboard exterior, pink neon lights and an assortment of interior decorative accents that harken back to the 1950s. Mountain View Diners of Little Falls/Singac built the car (serial no. 390). Originally known as the Atlantic Diner, it opened on June 15, 1963. In later years, it was known as Big Ernie's Diner. Hotel owners Eleftherios (his name means "liberty") and Eleni Katsanis purchased the diner and property in October 2004. "My son and daughter wanted the diner to have a 1950s theme. They picked the name," Eleftherios said. The diner reopened as the Pink Cadillac on June 6, 2005, and three years later, Eleftherios started leasing out the daily operations.

Originally from the ancient city of Mytilene, located on the Greek island of Lesbos, Eleftherios came to the United States when he was eleven years old. He earned a PhD degree at Clarkson University, New York, and made his mark in nanoscience chemistry. In 1985, he and his wife became investors in the Wildwood real estate market, buying and revitalizing three hotels and other properties, including the diner. When asked why he felt it was important to restore and maintain the diner, he sat back, smiled and confessed to being a proud Doo Wop enthusiast. "The diner is authentic, not modernized," he stressed. "We've lost a lot of our Doo Wop culture here in Wildwood. That's why I wanted to keep the diner original."

# A Tree and a Diner with Sturdy Roots

Robert McAllister hit it big in the spring of 1955 at Brandywine Raceway, a harness track located outside Wilmington, Delaware. He took his $34,000 in winnings and decided that it was time to fulfill a dream. Barbara McAllister, Robert's daughter-in-law, said the dream was to own and operate a diner with his wife, Olivia. Now he had the funds to move forward with his plan and did so enthusiastically. At the time, Robert worked as a deliveryman, bringing pies, cakes and other baked goods to luncheonettes and restaurants throughout Salem County. He contacted Silk City and placed his order, which turned out to be a diner car with the serial no. 5512. The Salem Oak Diner, located on West Broadway in Salem, was delivered via a flat-bed tractor trailer and celebrated its grand opening on Wednesday, September 21, 1955.

The eatery's name was a tip of the hat to the giant Salem Oak, one of New Jersey's most iconic trees, which stood in the Friends Burial Grounds (established in 1676) on West Broadway, across the street from the diner. An original menu from the diner's opening day offers a glimpse of the business scene in the mid-1950s: $0.10 for coffee; $0.30 for a stack of pancakes; $0.70 for two eggs with ham, bacon or sausage, with sides of potatoes and toast; $0.60 for a double hamburger special with French fries; $0.90 for fried fillet of flounder, $1.15 for a roast turkey platter; and $2.00 for a broiled tenderloin steak.

McAllister's Salem Oak Diner enjoyed immediate success due to the region's solid middle-class customer base. During his days as a delivery man, he scrutinized the lay of the land and came to the conclusion that a well-run diner could fill a niche and become a profitable business. This corner of New Jersey boomed in the 1950s thanks to business development from a diversified industrial base: DuPont (chemicals and gunpowder), Heinz (food products), Anchor Hocking and Gayner (glass), Mannington Mills (floor coverings and carpets) and Atlantic City Electric (power generation). Salem bustled as area residents enjoyed the benefits of reliable factory jobs.

Salem Oak Tree. *Photo by M. Gabriele.*

The Salem Oak served customers twenty-four hours a day, seven days a week. After a year in business, the diner expanded to add a much-needed larger kitchen and dishwashing area. "All the industries we had in Salem County were good for business, but the work became very demanding," Barbara recalled, adding that her father-in-law had a strong commitment to the diner, worked long hours and rarely took time off for vacations or holidays. "My father-in-law was the happiest man in the world when he had the Salem Oak. He used to say that owning a diner won't make you rich, but you'll make a decent living and never go hungry. But someone always had to be there," she said, meaning a member of the family.

Barbara, who grew up in Penns Grove, began dating McAllister's son, Robert Jr. (Bob), during their teenage days. Bob served in the navy, and after he returned, they married in 1959. He worked at the diner, and Barbara had a job with New Jersey Bell. In late 1959, Bill Harris hired Bob to open the Deepwater Diner in Carneys Point, but after two years, Bob left the Deepwater and worked at DuPont for nearly five years before returning to the family's diner business in Salem.

By the mid-1960s, Olivia and Robert's health had begun to decline. Bob and Barbara purchased the Salem Oak and took over the business on June 1, 1966. Robert McAllister died in April 1972, while Olivia passed away in March 1984. The diner remained profitable under the steady ownership of Barbara and Bob, but the business environment in Salem County during the 1970s and 1980s began to deteriorate due to corporate downsizing and deindustrialization. Heinz and DuPont shuttered facilities and laid off workers. Ardagh Glass (formerly known as Anchor Hocking) closed its plant in Salem in October 2014.

The years eventually took their toll on the McAllister family. Bob suffered a stroke in 2005, which forced him and Barbara to quit the business. Barbara said that May 14, 2006, was their farewell day at the diner. Their four sons maintained the diner for another year, but the family knew it was time to let go and sell the diner. "It just became too much for us," Barbara said. The Salem Oak went through two different sets of owners until the current proprietor, Cafer Yardim, took over in November 2013. Born in Giresun, Turkey, a city along the Black Sea coast, he came to New Jersey in 1996 and worked at the Quinton Diner in Salem (currently Andy's Restaurant) and the Golden Pigeon Diner in Bridgeton, before landing at the Salem Oak.

Time, the elements and gravity took their toll on the six-hundred-year-old Salem Oak. The massive tree fell without warning on Thursday,

Salem Oak Diner. *Photo by M. Gabriele.*

June 6, 2019. The colossus, one of New Jersey's great natural monuments, is no longer part of the landscape.

The wizened Salem Oak Diner, still displaying the pink and blue colors on its stainless steel façade, is a survivor. "The diner has a devoted line of customers," Salem resident Cathy Lanard said when asked to explain why the Salem Oak has weathered the turbulent economic conditions of the region. Although she loves to cook, Cathy and her husband, Robert, regularly dine at the Salem Oak. She joked that the old-timers affectionately refer to the Salem Oak as "Rumor Central."

The Salem Oak Tree, prior to its demise, and the Salem Oak Diner were neighbors that anchored this southwestern corner of New Jersey. Today, the diner stands alone. Barbara said that it's her dream that the diner remains open and stays true to its original Silk City architectural design. "It's important to me because diners were my life."

# "I EQUATE MEMORIES WITH LIFE"

**W**hat does the future hold for diners in the beautiful state of New Jersey? There are hundreds of diner stories that have been lost or forgotten. There are hundreds of diner stories yet to be told. This book has documented some of them—a collection of sketches that records people, places and events in motion.

Richard Gutman of West Roxbury, Massachusetts, receives calls from journalists and academics on a regular basis. The question he's most frequently asked is: why are so many diners disappearing? It's a question that reflects concerns over the sustainability of the diner business model in the twenty-first century. However, Gutman—having studied diner history for more than four decades—rejects the premise of the question.

"I disagree. They're not disappearing," Gutman declared, saying that understanding the grand sweep of the American diner and lunch wagon business during the last 147 years means understanding its constant growth and evolution. "We do lose diners and some do change. Not everything can be saved, but this is the natural progression of business. We'll always have small, vintage diners."

Gutman said that these days he's "more open to how we define a 'real diner.' Diners today can be hard to categorize. But each diner has its own personality. There's nothing else like them." In a feature on Garden State diners penned by this author for the May 2018 edition of *New Jersey Monthly* magazine, Gutman was quoted as a key source for the story. He said that diners have always been places where people go to share ideas. "It's part of a diner's mystique. It's something that goes beyond food." When it comes to pinpointing a diner's essence, he considers whether the eatery has a meaningful place in the community it serves. He also reconfirmed that New Jersey remains the Diner Capital of the World. "Without a doubt," he said.

Beth Lennon is an author and social media entrepreneur committed to documenting Americana treasures. Lennon's alter ego, Mod Betty, is a perky, retro romantic "travel hostess." Beth's (and Mod Betty's) interests range from diners to duckpin bowling, grand movie theaters, neighborhood bakeries and ice cream parlors, frozen custard stands, rodeos and numerous other homespun cultural ports of call—"places that give you a step-back-in-time feeling."

Lennon's Retro Roadmap website, which features Mod Betty's adventures, was launched as a blog post in 2009 and informs readers about attractions that she feels deserve to be better known and appreciated, like vintage diners. As defined in her website's mission statement, she's doing her part to celebrate authentic places that have stood the test of time and kept their original charm. The key phase is "stood the test of time." Lennon admires those who work hard to keep their retro treasures viable and relevant. "People lament when a favorite spot closes in their community. I want people to get excited and support the business before it closes."

What will happen to classic diners that are points of interest on the Retro Roadmap? "That's a tough question," she admitted, choosing her words carefully. "When I see a 'mom and pop' family owned diner, and there's a next generation ready to take over, then that's a good sign. It's also a good sign when the diner family owns the property." Lennon added that it's not a good sign when she sees mom and pop businesses that have become "grandma and grandpop businesses," with no one waiting in the wings.

In her hometown of Phoenixville, Pennsylvania, she and her fellow residents witnessed the end of an era in the spring of 2017 when the Vale-Rio Diner—a sleek 1948, Jersey-built Paramount car—was wrapped in plastic and taken away by a tractor trailer truck. According to Lennon's blog and local online news reports, the diner had been a Phoenixville favorite before it closed in 2008. Three years earlier, the presence of the Vale-Rio Diner factored into her family's decision to move to Phoenixville. "This was a loss to our town's collective history."

Photographer extraordinaire Larry Cultrera of Saugus, Massachusetts, the author of *New Hampshire Diners*, *Classic Granite State Eateries* and *Classic Diners of Massachusetts* and the editor behind the *Diner Hotline* blog, snapped his first diner picture on the morning of Saturday, November 29,

1980. He took a photograph of the By-Pass Diner (today known as the American Dream Diner), located in Harrisburg, Pennsylvania, and built by DeRaffele. "I took only one shot of the diner, but that was the pivotal shot," he said, referring to how it sparked his passionate study of diners. Ever since that day, he's been hooked, and his cameras have captured more than 860 diners throughout New Jersey, Pennsylvania, New England and elsewhere—a most valuable photo archive.

Considering his seasoned eye for roadside attractions, I asked him to step back and describe, philosophically, what he has documented over the last thirty-nine years. What does he see when he reviews his photos? What's revealed in the grand sum of his pictures? "I think about the memories I've photographed. I equate memories with life." His photos also capture a sense of place—the settings that frame a diner's location. "When I'm taking pictures, I think about the diner in conjunction with everything else that surrounds it."

MEMORIES TRIGGERED BY DINERS become indelible reference points. One diner memory stands out for Cultrera—a memory he didn't capture with his camera. In the mid-1980s, he stopped for breakfast at the Agawam Diner in Rowley, Massachusetts, a diner manufactured in New Jersey by Fodero. The joint was packed and the atmosphere lively when in walked a lone hitchhiker—a gaunt young man with a scruffy beard and tattered clothes. Based on his appearance, it was clear that this troubled chap's soul had logged many difficult miles.

Seated at the counter, Cultrera overheard the conversation that ensued. Speaking to the diner owners, the hitchhiker offered to clean up the parking lot and do a few other chores in exchange for a hot meal. The diner owners responded immediately. "Please son, sit down," they said to him. "What do you need?" There was no mention of chores. The hitchhiker was well fed, an act of kindness that sustained him. He finished his meal and went on his way.

"I saw the diner spirit that day," Cultrera said, telling the story with a lift in his voice, as though it had happened yesterday. It's a spirit that transcends geographic boundaries for people who love diners.

WHEN IT COMES TO appreciating a diner's spirit and its place in a community, Anthony Natale, whose family ran the White Crystal Diner in Atlantic Highlands for forty years, said it best: "The story of any diner

Tick Tock Diner, sunrise, Christmas Day 2018. *Photo by M. Gabriele.*

is the customers. I shared a lot with my customers—good times and bad. My customers were like family. They were people from all walks of life. It wasn't easy for me to say goodbye."

New Jersey can commemorate the accomplishments of its long-gone, prolific diner manufacturers—the companies and stouthearted workers who designed and built the magical stainless steel structures that are admired throughout the world. The state can laud diner owners and employees for their hard work, dedication, hospitality and culinary skills and celebrate the loyal patrons in the state's twenty-one counties that support this beloved enterprise.

There always will be more diners to discover and memories to savor—in New Jersey and beyond. Traditions evolve, menus change and a new era of ownership is unfolding, but the Garden State has renowned, time-tested favorites that anchor the state's diner circuit, with new eateries in the pipeline and on the drawing board. Diners and all that they represent, as cultural monuments and inviting places to eat and meet, will remain part of New Jersey's landscape.

C'mon, Harvey, let's get some breakfast. My treat.

# SOURCES

*Books*

Baeder, John. *Diners*. New York: Harry N. Abrams, 1978.

Baptista, Robert J. *Elizabeth, New Jersey: Then and Now*. Orange, TX: self-published, 2015. Online version at https://archive.org/details/ElizabethNewJerseyThenAndNowSecondEdition2015.

Barth, Linda J. *The Delaware and Raritan Canal*. Images of America. Charleston, SC: Arcadia Publishing, 2002.

Cunningham, John T. *New Jersey: America's Main Road*. Garden City, NY: Doubleday and Company. 1966.

———. *This Is New Jersey*. New Brunswick, NJ: Rutgers University Press, 1994.

Edwards, Richard. *Industries of New Jersey: Trenton, Princeton, Hightstown, Pennington and Hopewell*. Part 1: *Industries of New Jersey*. New York: Historical Publishing Company, 1882.

Flack, John S., Jr. *Evesham Township*. Images of America. Charleston, SC: Arcadia Publishing, 2012.

Gabriele, Michael C. *The History of Diners in New Jersey*. Charleston, SC: The History Press, 2013.

Genovese, Peter. *Jersey Diners*. New Brunswick, NJ: Rutgers University Press, 1996.

Gutman, Richard J.S. *American Diner Then & Now*. Baltimore, MD: Johns Hopkins University Press, 2000.

Hirsch, Anita S. *Wildwood by the Sea: Nostalgia and Recipes*. Wildwood, NJ: Holly Beach Press, 2009.

*History of Monmouth County, New Jersey, 1664–1920. Vol. 3.* N.p. Lewis Historical Publishing Company. Google Books, online text, 1922.

Ingraham, Arjorie Monidis, and the Vineland Historical and Antiquarian Society. *Vineland.* Postcard History Series. Charleston, SC: Arcadia Publishing, 2014.

Lee, Francis Bazley. *Genealogical and Personal Memorial of Mercer County, New Jersey.* New York: Lewis Publishing Company, 1907.

National Reporter System—United States Series. *The Federal Reporter.* Vol. 179: *Cases Argued and Determined in the Circuit Courts of Appeals and Circuit and District Courts of the United States.* N.p.: West Publishing Company 1910.

Pizzi, Jenna, and Susan Sprague Yeske. *The Pork Roll Cookbook.* Kennebunkport, ME: Cider Mill Press, 2015.

Podmore, Harry J. *Trenton Old and New.* Trenton, NJ: Kenneth W. Moore, 1927. Updated by the Trenton Tercentenary Commission in 1964. Online at http://www.trentonhistory.org.

Regan, Timothy E. *Keyport in the Twentieth Century.* The American Century Series. Charleston, SC: Arcadia Publishing, 1998.

Twain, Mark. *Roughing It.* Hartford, CT: American Publishing Company, 1872.

Williams, Jay. *John Baeder's Road Well Taken.* New York: Vendome Press, 2015.

Yorke, Douglas A., Jr., John Margolies and Eric Baker. *Hitting the Road: The Art of the American Road Map.* San Francisco, CA: Chronicle Books, 1996.

## City Directories

Bloomfield City Directory, 1910, 1959, 1961 and others.
East Newark Director, 1938.
Montclair City Directory, 1930 and others.
Newark City Directory, 1934, 1974, 1976.
Red Bank City Director, 1956, 1958–59.
Summit City Directory, 1905, 1909, 1913 1916, 1930 and others.

## Libraries, Government Offices, Historical Societies and Museums

Atlantic City Free Public Library.
Blairstown Historical Society.
Bloomfield Public Library.

Bound Brook Public Library.
Burlington County Historical Society.
Burlington County Library System.
Clifton Public Library.
Cornelius Low House Museum, Piscataway.
Cranford Historical Society.
Cranford Public Library.
Egg Harbor City Historical Society.
Evesham Library.
Evesham Township, Community Development Coordinator Janice Koch.
George F. Boyer Historical Museum, Wildwood Historical Society.
Green Brook Historical Society (Denise Wolf).
Historical Society of Bloomfield.
Jewish Historical Society of New Jersey, Whippany.
Lambert Castle Museum, Paterson.
Library of Congress, Washington, D.C.
Montclair History Center.
Montclair Public Library.
Morris Museum, Morristown.
Morristown and Morris Township Library, Morristown.
Newark Public Library, Charles F. Cummings New Jersey Information Center.
Nutley Historical Society.
Nutley Public Library.
Red Bank Public Library.
Summit Free Public Library.
Summit Historical Society.
Sussex County Historical Society, Newton.
Trenton Free Public Library.
Verona Public Library.
Vineland Antiquarian and Historical Society.

## *Magazines*

*The American Restaurant* (December 1921).
*Grand Rapids Business Journal* (August 29, 2017).
*Grand Rapids Magazine* (May 18, 2018).
*New Jersey Monthly* (May 2018). Cover story on diners by M. Gabriele.
*The New Yorker* (March 25, 2017).

*The New York Times Magazine* (February 7, 1926).
*Parade Magazine* (March 11, 1945).
*The Poultry Monthly Magazine* (January 1883).
*The Progressive Age* (July 15, 1910).
*South Jersey Magazine* (July 2014).
*Time Out Magazine* (Sunday, April 2, 2017).

## Museum Exhibits (co-curated by M. Gabriele)

Cornelius Low House/Middlesex County Museum, Piscataway. "The History of New Jersey Diners." April 12, 2015–June 26, 2016.

Lambert Castle, Paterson. "Pancakes, Patties and Pies: The History of the Silk City Diner Company of Paterson." August 6–October 5, 2014.

Morris Museum, Morristown. "Icons of American Culture: The History of New Jersey Diners." September 9–December 31, 2016.

## Newspapers

*Atlantic City Press*. June 1, 1960.
*Bayshore News* (Keyport). February 16, 1953.
*Beach Haven Times*. May 6, 1959.
*Blairstown Press*. September 1958 and September 29, 1949.
*Camden Daily Courier*. Several articles, including April 11, 1901, and June 15, 1915.
*Courier-News*. Numerous articles.
*Courier-Post*. February 6, 1983, February 7, 1963.
*Cranford Citizen and Chronicle*. Numerous articles.
*Daily Journal*. June 2, 2015; April 15, 2015; June 23, 1992; June 29, 1992; and other articles.
*Daily Targum* (Rutgers University, New Brunswick, NJ). Online articles, February 28, 2018, and January 31, 2017.
*Elizabeth Daily Journal*. Numerous articles.
*Grand Rapids Press*. February 12, 1993.
*Hammonton Gazette*. March 21, 2018.
*Herald-News*. September 19, 1933; May 31, 1977; and March 13, 1981
*Hub* (Red Bank). August 29, 2003.
*Independent* (Keyport). April 2, 1986, and September 1991.

*Independent Press.* April 22, 1954.

*Independent Press and Bloomfield Citizen.* August 13, 1915.

*Jersey Journal.* August 28, 2003, and December 27, 1946.

*Leader* (Wildwood/Cape May). August 9, 2006; June 13, 1963; and March 31, 1955.

*Mainland Journal.* January 25, 1973.

*Middlesex Chronicle.* June 10, 1965.

*Montclair Times.* November 4, 1943.

*Mount Holly Herald.* March 1960.

*Newark Call.* January 1914.

*Newark Evening News.* Numerous articles.

*Newark Sunday News.* June 22, 1969.

*New York Times.* Numerous articles.

*Passaic Daily News.* March 2, 1895, and other articles.

*Philadelphia Inquirer.* August 27, 2017.

*Poughkeepsie Journal.* October 15, 2015.

*Press of Atlantic City.* July 2, 2014, and July 2009.

*Ramsey Journal.* Various articles, 1954 and 1955.

*Record.* January 30, 2017, and February 4, 1993.

*Ridgewood News.* October 3, 1996.

*Star-Ledger.* Numerous articles.

*Summit Herald.* May 17, 1979, and other articles.

*Sunday Times-Advertiser.* August 11, 1946.

*Trenton Evening Times.* February 1, 1914, and February 11, 1909.

*Trenton Sunday Times-Advertiser.* May 6, 1928, and August 11, 1946.

*Trenton Times.* May 24, 2014.

*Union News Daily.* June 9, 2018.

*Verona-Cedar Grove Times.* September 9, 1976, and May 26, 1955.

*Vineland Daily Journal.* June 29, 1992; June 23, 1992; July 20, 1988.

*Vineland Evening Times.* October 31, 1941, and January 5, 1939.

## *Online Articles, Blogs and Websites*

American Diner Durlach. https://diner-durlach.de.

*Bergen Record.* northjersey.com.

Bodian, Nat. Old Newark. www.oldnewark.com.

Camden New Jersey, Olga's Diner. www.dvrbs.com.

Case's Pork Roll Company. www.caseporkrollnj.com.

# SOURCES

Courier Post Online. www.courierpostonline.com.

Cultrera, Larry. *Diner Hotline Weblog*. https://dinerhotline.wordpress.com.

*Daily Record*. www.dailyrecord.com.

Ellis, Tieka. Selective Potential. www.selectivepotential.com.

Facebook (various posts).

Greenwood Magnetics. "Properties of 304 Stainless Steel." www.greenwoodmagnetics.com.

Guide to Atlantic City. "Early Atlantic City Nightclubs." www.monopolycity.com.

Harwin, Steve. Diversified Diners. www.diversifieddiners.com.

*Historical and Industrial Review of Camden, New Jersey*. New York: Commercial Publishing Company, New York, 1890. Online version of business journal. http://www.dvrbs.com.

Historical Society of Elizabeth. "Singer Sewing Machine Company." www.visithistoricalelizabethnj.org.

Historical Society of Ocean Grove. oceangrovehistory.org.

Jewish Link of North Jersey. January 26, 2017. www.jewishlinknj.com.

Koennemann, Kristen. Only in Your State: New Jersey. www.onlyinyourstate.com.

Levittown Beyond. http://www.levittownbeyond.com.

Lindheimer, Kelly. History Girl. www.thehistorygirl.com.

"Mt. Holly Area, Yesterday and Today." Facebook group page.

My Central Jersey. www.mycentraljersey.com.

My Verona, NJ. www.myveronanj.com.

New Jersey Food Truck Association. www.njfta.org.

New Jersey Hills Media Group. www.newjerseyhills.com.

New Jersey Isn't Boring. http://newjerseyisntboring.com.

New Jersey Online. nj.com.

New Jersey Weather and Climate Network. www.njweather.org.

Newspapers.com.

*Philadelphia Inquirer* and *Daily News*. July 31, 2013. philly.com.

*Philadelphia Inquirer*. https://www.inquirer.com.

Retro Roadmap with Mod Betty. www.retroroadmap.com.

RU Hungry? www.ruhungrynj.net.

Sauers, Richard A., Riverview Cemetery Historian's Blogspot. https://riverviewcemetery.blogspot.com.

Schmidt, Barbara. Twain Quotes. http://www.twainquotes.com.

Singer Sewing Machine Information Site. "Singer Factories: Elizabethport, New Jersey, USA." www.singersewinginfo.co.uk/elizabethport.

Smith, Deborah, and Rachel Bozek. Jersey Bites. https://jerseybites.com.

Thrillist. www.thrillist.com.

Train Sights On. "Singer Sewing Machine Company." www.ericwilliamsblog. com.

Truck Stop Diner, Kearny, NJ. http://www.truckstopdinernj.com.

Weequahic High School Alumni Association. http://weequahicalumni.org.

Wikipedia. www.wikipedia.org.

Wildwood Video Archive. http://wildwoodvideoarchive.com.

WSOC TV news, Charlotte, NC. www.wsoctv.com.

Yelp. www.yelp.com.

## *Miscellaneous*

Bernarducci Art Gallery, 525 West 25th Street, New York, New York. www. bernarduccigallery.com.

*Bizarre Foods with Andrew Zimmern*. Segment on Shelby, North Carolina livermush, May 5, 2009.

Borenstein, Paula. Notes of her February 2007 interview with Louise Bauman.

Charter of the City of Paterson, Edmund G. Stalter, 1908. Paterson, NJ: News Printing Company, State Printers. https://books.google.com.

*Diners, Drive-Ins and Dives*. Segment on the Bayway Diner, July 23, 2007.

Green Brook Fire Department ledger book. Courtesy of Jack de Rosset.

*Harvey*. Universal International Pictures, December 21, 1950. Based on the 1944 play by Mary Chase.

James Beard Foundation Award, 2009. Information and certificate displayed at Mustache Bill's Diner, West Eighth Street, Barnegat Light, New Jersey.

New Jersey Department of Environmental Protection, Office of New Jersey Heritage. Historical Sites Inventory No. 2018, no. 2610. Provided by the Summit Historical Society.

Obama, President Barack. Commencement speech at Rutgers University, New Brunswick, New Jersey, May 15, 2016. https://obamawhitehouse. archives.gov/the-press-office.

Persson, Jess P. World War II draft registration card.

*Progressive Age (Gas, Electricity and Water)*. A New York business journal. July 15, 1910. Available at https://books.google.com.

Riverview Cemetery, 870 Centre Street, Trenton, New Jersey. Facebook page available at www.facebook.com/RiverviewCemeteryTrentonNJ.

Stavros Inc. Deed, October 28, 1959. Provided by Evesham Township via an "open public records act request form." http://www.evesham-nj.org.

United States Department of the Interior, National Park Service. National Register of Historic Places Registration Form, NPS Form 10-900, October 1990. Summit Downtown Historic District.

## *Diner/Wagon Manufacturers Mentioned in the Text*

Campora Dining Car Company, Kearny.

DeRaffele Manufacturing Company, New Rochelle, New York.

Fitzgibbon and Crisp's Union Carriage Works, Trenton.

Fodero Dining Car Company, Bloomfield. Briefly known as National Dining Car Company, Newark.

Jerry O'Mahony Inc., (Bayonne) Elizabeth.

J.J. Hennigan, Worcester, Massachusetts.

Kullman Dining Car Company, Newark and Harrison. Later became known as Kullman Industries Inc., Avenel and Lebanon.

Mahony Diners Inc., Kearny.

Manno Dining Car Company, (Belleville) Fairfield.

Master Diners, Pequannock.

Mountain View Diners, Singac/Little Falls.

Paramount Dining Car Company, Haledon.

Patrick J. Tierney Company, New Rochelle, New York.

P.J. Tierney Sons Inc., New Rochelle, New York.

PMC Diners Inc., Oakland.

Silk City Diners, a Division of the Paterson Vehicle Company, Paterson.

Superior Dining Car Company, Berlin.

Swingle Diners Inc., Middlesex.

T.H. Buckley Car Manufacturing Company, Worcester, Massachusetts.

United Diner Construction Inc., Philadelphia, Pennsylvania.

United Diner Manufacturing Company, Newark.

Worcester Lunch Car and Carriage Manufacturing Company, Worcester, Massachusetts.

# INDEX

# ABOUT THE AUTHOR

*Photo by Megan Fleischer.*

T his is Michael C. Gabriele's fourth book on New Jersey history, all published by The History Press. The previous books are (in chronological order): *The Golden Age of Bicycle Racing in New Jersey*, *The History of Diners in New Jersey* and *New Jersey Folk Revival Music: History and Tradition*. A lifelong Garden State resident, he is a 1975 graduate of Montclair State University and has worked as a journalist, freelance writer and author for more than forty years. Gabriele is a member of the board of trustees for the annual New Jersey Folk Festival at Rutgers University, a member of the executive board for the Nutley Historical Society and serves on the advisory board of the Clifton Arts Center. He writes an occasional diner blog for the website Jersey Bites: A Quest for Food with Attitude (https://jerseybites.com) and enjoys exploring the diverse regions of the Garden State.